TIME AND PLACE
✦
WEST AND EAST

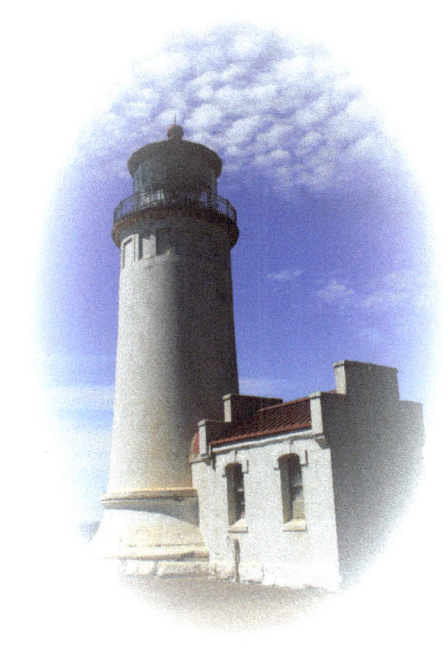

TIME AND PLACE
◆
WEST AND EAST

Jim and Carol McCord

SHANTI ARTS PUBLISHING
BRUNSWICK, MAINE

TIME AND PLACE ✦ WEST AND EAST

Copyright © 2024 Jim and Carol McCord

All Rights Reserved

Published by Shanti Arts Publishing

Designed by Shanti Arts Designs

All photographs by Carol McCord except for the following: (p. 88) "The Industrious Cottager" by Jim McCord; (p. 164) "Maui" by Jim McCord; and (p. 167) "Thai Leaves" by Dave Stamoulis / alamy.com. All photographs used with permission of the artist.

Shanti Arts LLC
193 Hillside Road
Brunswick, Maine 04011
shantiarts.com

Printed in the United States of America

ISBN: 978-1-962082-30-3 (softcover)
ISBN: 978-1-962082-34-1 (hardcover)

Library of Congress Control Number: 2024939911

For all who know
"Nature is not a place to visit, it is home."

"I do not pretend to understand Nature, but I get on very well with her in a neighborly way."

—Rupert Brooke

CONTENTS

Acknowledgments	13
PROLOGUE	
Waters	17
WEST	
Olympic Coastal Forest	20
Raykovich's Grandfather	22
Neah Bay	24
Oysterville Dawn	27
Oysterville	29
After Death	30
Long Beach Lichen	32
Orb Web	35
Bay View Spruce	37
Clump of Seaweed on the Longest Beach in the World	38
Reading a Sand Dollar	40
Hanging Shells near Kehoe Beach	43
Picture Window View	45
Morro Bay	46
Winter Out the Back of Marsh Cottage	49
Romancing on Tomales Bay	51
Snowy Plover	52
In Defense of Devil's Ivy	54
White Hibiscus	56
Amaryllis	59
Sunflowers	61
Two Daylilies	63
The Smell of Flowers and Wood	64
Raku Vase	67
Diurnal	69
Lake at Dusk	70
Lake at Dawn	72

EAST

Names and Places 1984	76
Skunk Cabbage in Our Wetlands	80
Upstate	82
Spring Pond near Saratoga	85
2.6 Suburban Acres	87
The Industrious Cottager	89
Advice to a Painter of Still Lifes	90
Natural History	92
Serpent in Our Garden	94
Tree Hopper	97
Felled	99
Mercy Killing	101
Hadley Mountain Fire Watch Late Summer	102
Blue Heron	104
Autumn	106
October Gardening	109
Mixed Music	111
Near Gibby's Diner	112
Thanksgiving at Saltsman's Hotel	114
Bulb Planting	116
Harping in New Lebanon	119
In the Field	121
Red-Tailed	123
Murder in the Graveyard	124
Momentary Alignment	126
Lightning Strike	128
Even Oak	131
Retreat	133
First Snow in the Pine Barren	135
Ill-Tempered Prayer	137
Orchard Plans	138

WEST AND EAST

The Difficulty of Dividing Day from Night	142
Eyeing the Sea	144
Late Summer Blues	147
Lesson for Survival	149
Winter Downtown	150
A Winter Tale	152
Death's Life Span	155
Pitch Pine	156
Unused Red Barn	158
Man of Sorrows	160
Recovery	163
Maui	165
Thai Leaves	166
Night and Day near Cape Disappointment	168
Suburban Deer	171
The Forest Refuge in January	172
Biographies	175

ACKNOWLEDGMENTS

Early versions of a selection of poems unaccompanied by photographs appeared in *Approaching Winter Solstice, Bittern Sweet,* and *Building Relationships: Selected Works of Jim McCord and Bruce McColl.* Several photographs unaccompanied by poems appeared in these exhibitions and journal: Albany Pine Bush, Arkell Museum, Connecticut Academy of Fine Arts, Biennial of Fine Art & Documentary Photography, Julia Margaret Cameron Award for Women Photographers, Kelly Adirondack Center, *Still Point Arts Quarterly.*

We're deeply grateful to Annette LeClair, Harry Marten, and Bunkong Tuon for their generous and valued comments on both photos and poems over many years. Our special thanks, too, to Kelly Collett, Jackie Craven, David Kaczynski, Ginit Marten, Eric McCord, Shawne McCord, Dan Payne, and Malcolm Willison for their thoughtful critiques and kind support.

Our very special thanks to Christine Cote for the attention and loving care she gives to all she does as writer, editor, designer, and publisher at Shanti Arts.

PROLOGUE

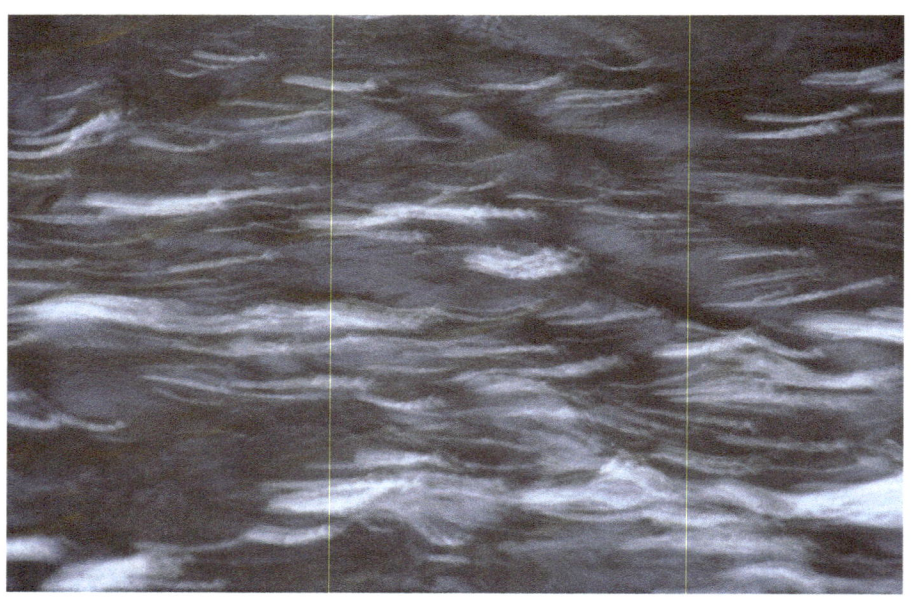

WATERS

As west coast kids our spring-fed lakes
glowed with grass and reeds, lapped
like gentle incoming tides. Our rivers
flowed like hearts in perfect rhythm,
rippled to caress pebbled beds. Our ocean
swells soothed, its breakers thrilled.

As newcomers to the east we saw lakes toxic,
fouled rivers snake their way through narrow
valleys and rock-infested woodlands of dead
trees, raging waters turn streets into canals,
turn houses into splintered crates. We felt
the ocean sweat in summer, convulse in winter.

Biases at cross currents like a maelstrom.

WEST

OLYMPIC COASTAL FOREST

*"If you've seen one ... tree,
you've seen them all."*

—Ronald Reagan

Conifers wear different coats
in this wet part of the country:
double mackinaw for Douglas fir,
windbreakers for alder, fur-lined
for cedar. No two alike or isolate.
Broken branches expose joints
of deep-veined marble, charred
pockets of buoyant cork. Fallen
nurse logs nurture offshoots
waving like fly rods toward light,
dropping tentacles like anchors
to the herbaceous floor. Moss
hangs like drapery of carded wool
before it's spun to yarn. Hiking
steep stream banks one must strain
to see where clinging roots stop,
supporting rock begins. On the nearby
sandy shore at Kalaloch one squints
to not see beached trees as carcasses
of whales, bleached femurs and scapulae
beside shells etched like burrowing
beetle tracks, carpi scattered amidst
seaweed ribbed like cedar needles.

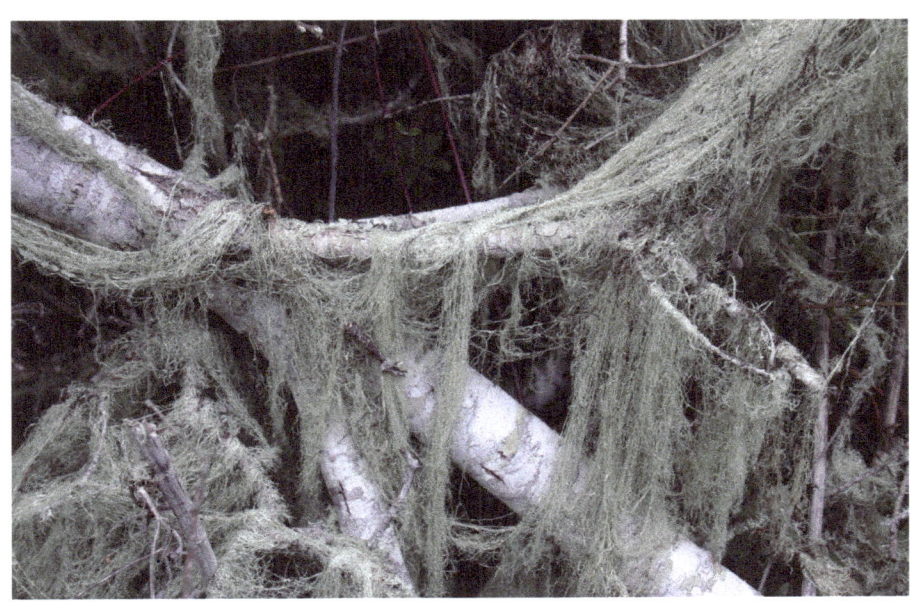

RAYKOVICH'S GRANDFATHER

Vukson Delevich cut Olympic pine
and Sitka spruce for forty years
in coarse wool shirts red as coals
in Cooky's cast-iron stove. Ate
in a cookhouse walled with antlers,
washed down meals with coffee
stronger than a bull chain, black
as starless night. By day he echoed
the measured din of first woodsmen
throwing chips, whittling shakes,
sculpting stump farms, at night
slept pressed in a ramshackle shack
with dreams of steel biting bark
and the fragrance of downed wood.

With winter snows belt-high
off he'd go to river towns with fired
expectations and an appetite for more
than food. His speech to the ladies
smoother than cream, his talk with men
saltier than the hash and pork in camp.
Then back to woods when clapboard
pinched. "Cut out" his shout
to his Slovak mate, "Get out"
his Sabbath song to oxen carting
timber to river banks for the log
drive down to Yesler's mill
for saloons and hotels, churches,
plank coffins and graveside crosses.

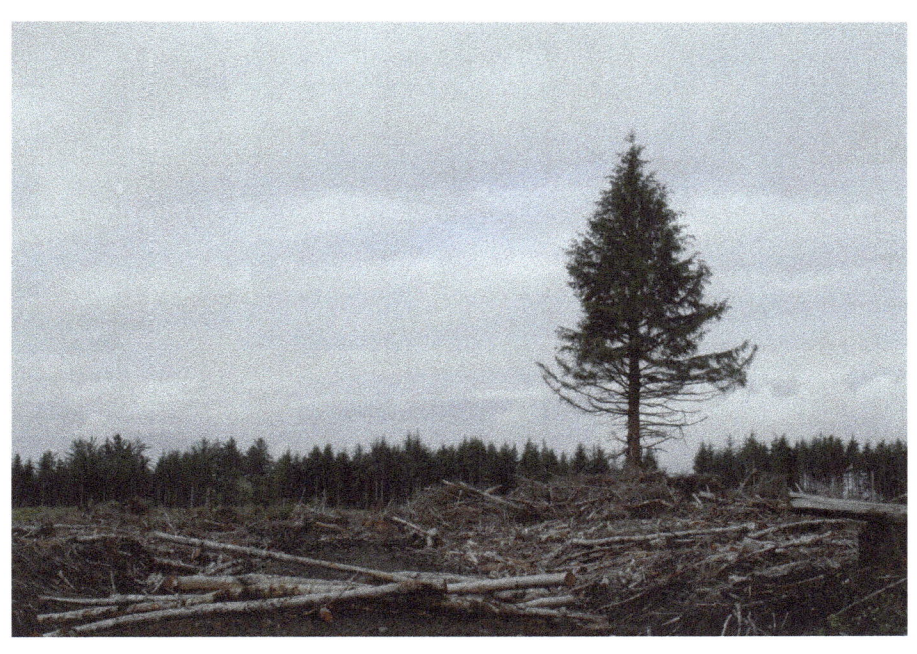

NEAH BAY

Under skies often gray as the seals
and whales that fed the Makah
thousands of years ago, hills
surrounding this fishing village
once held primary forests of yew,
cedar, spruce, hemlock, maple
thick as salmon during spawning run.

Today woodlands clear-cut, salmon
boats filled with summer tourists.

Here the land, not the sea, gave up
its dead. Dense hillsides now cemeteries
of stumps, biers of branches, briquette
mausoleums. In the distance white pines
once downed for masts prick remembrance
of brigs from Frisco trading smallpox
for the lives of 2/3rds of the tribe.

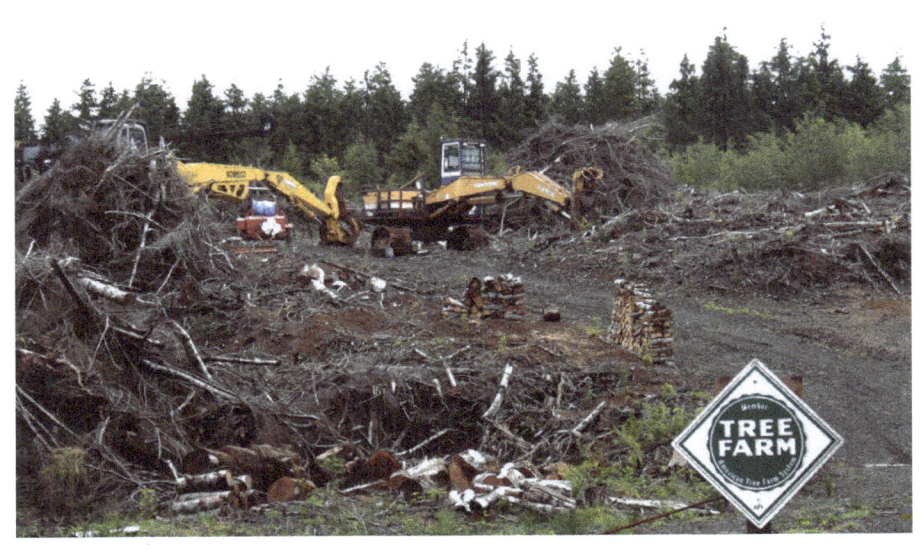

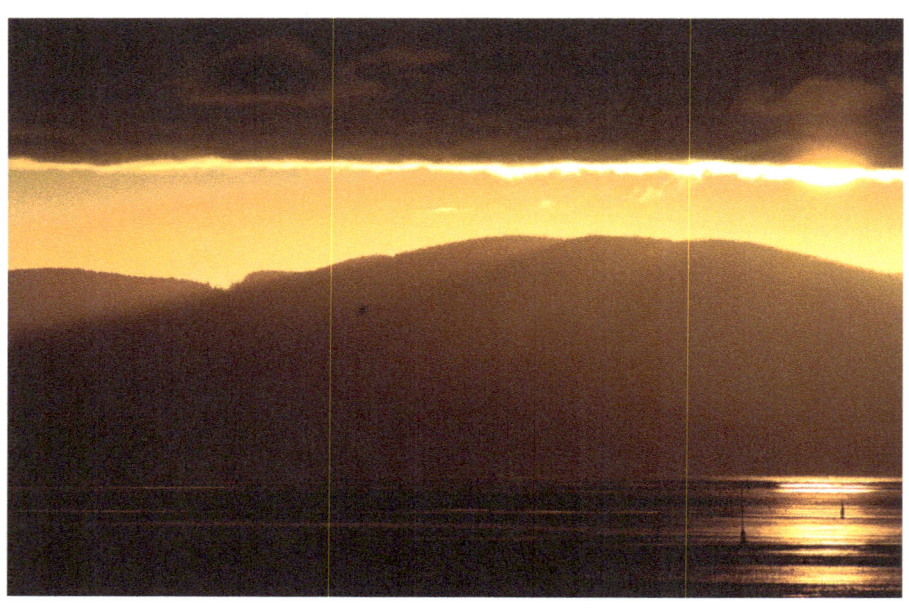

OYSTERVILLE DAWN

After a night of slow dancing,
stars give way to half-drawn
shades of light fluttering beneath
a ceiling of cloud. Fishing boats
slip toward sea along the chipped blade
of the knife that is east Long Beach.
Three tower lights across Willapa Bay
blink with fearless regularity.

As dawn brightens gulls crowd the sky
in unmapped flight. Some hang like gliders,
some jerk like kites on too tight strings,
some drift to ground like parachutes.
They accept what wind currents offer,
seem to know in their hollow bones
the forever shifting depths and shallows
of pools, the rise and fall of water
over mudflats and marshlands that tides
beget, nourish, and destroy.

I like to believe they also sense
in flight the constant tug of sun
and moon that makes our world wobble
always a little out of balance.

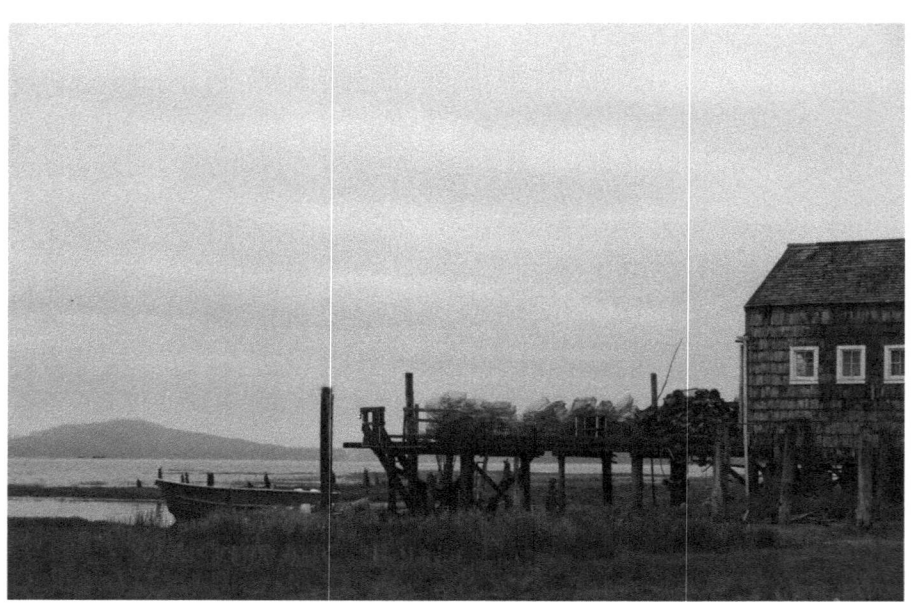

OYSTERVILLE

There's no still center here. Peace
radiates like the surface of its bay
when salmon jump and surrounds like waves
of sound that fade and can't be traced.

Historical moments filled and waned like lunar
phases—tempestuous in boom times of oyster
harvests, drinking, whoring—calm as still waters
after hotels folded, bars dried up, schools emptied.

Today no jetty dares separate fresh water
from saline or past from present. Life flows
like tides that only seem at rest, that shift
without ripples from out to in and in to out.

The village caressed by fertile, swaying
eel grass, protected by Mediterranean cypress
firmly fixed as fieldstone once stowed as ballast
on lumber schooners up from California.

AFTER DEATH

The village cemetery is packed
with Anglo monuments, headstones,
plaques sunk into grass hillocks
swelling like the ocean's chest.
A white man's genealogical
paradise of names and dates
in polished granite, planed wood,
common stone streaked with generations
of rain. The finest incised stones
shine like fashionable counter tops.
Biblical phrases bless a few, others
simply with identities that once
held meaning: husband, wife, child,
infant. Half a dozen family plots lie
under spruce whose canopies of darkness
spread each year. So foolish the Clarks,
the Espys, the Goulters to think white blood
lines have a chance against absent-minded
history. In the earliest corner the possible
site of Nahcati's grave. If there ever was
a Siwash burial canoe, it's long decayed
with chief's body, favorite wife, prize
possessions. A stalwart red cedar arches
over the hump of mound with carpet of shells.
The plot in a rectangular frame of uncut
stones placed surely, yet scattered,
as surely as Nahcati's spiritual union
with Willapa Bay, as scattered as his tribe
became when oystermen depleted it.

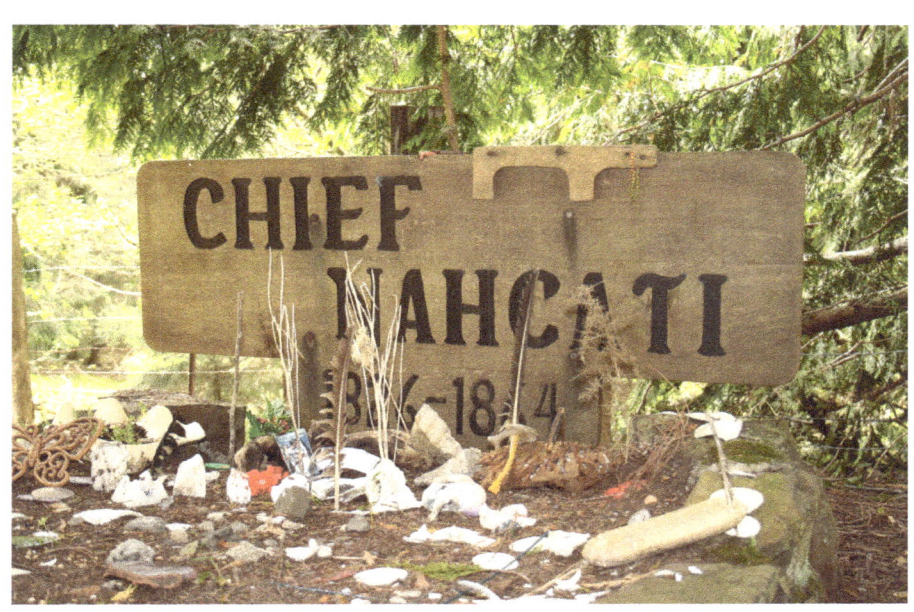

LONG BEACH LICHEN

Old Man's Beard on our picket fence
looks protective as lamb's wool
against blasts from the Pacific, looks
soft as plush lining of a Northwoods
jacket. But after a whiff of rot,
it sinks beak in, tears its carrion way
through oil-based paint, ravages
beauty-blessed wood, washes down xylem
with gulps of rain. A coastal devourer
as rapacious as a tidal flood without ebb.

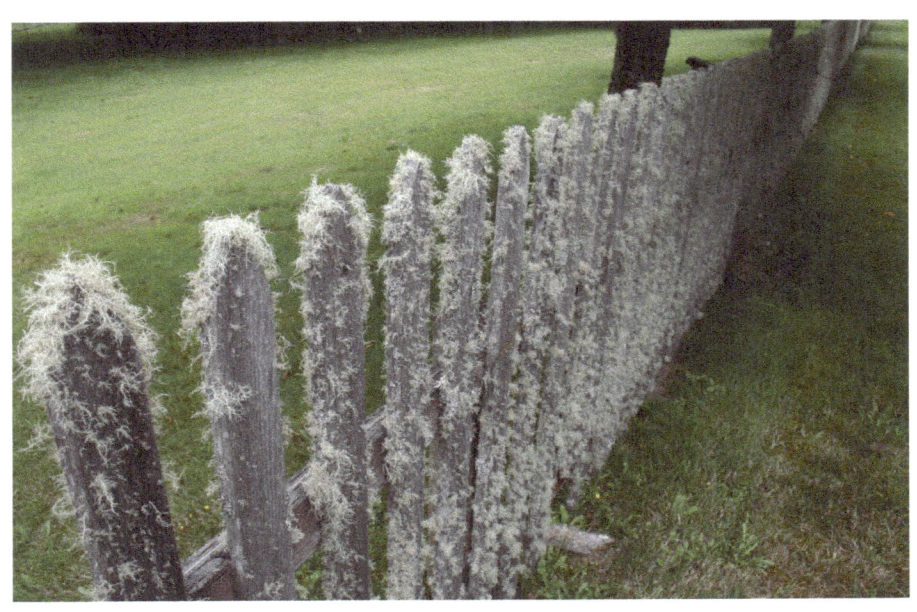

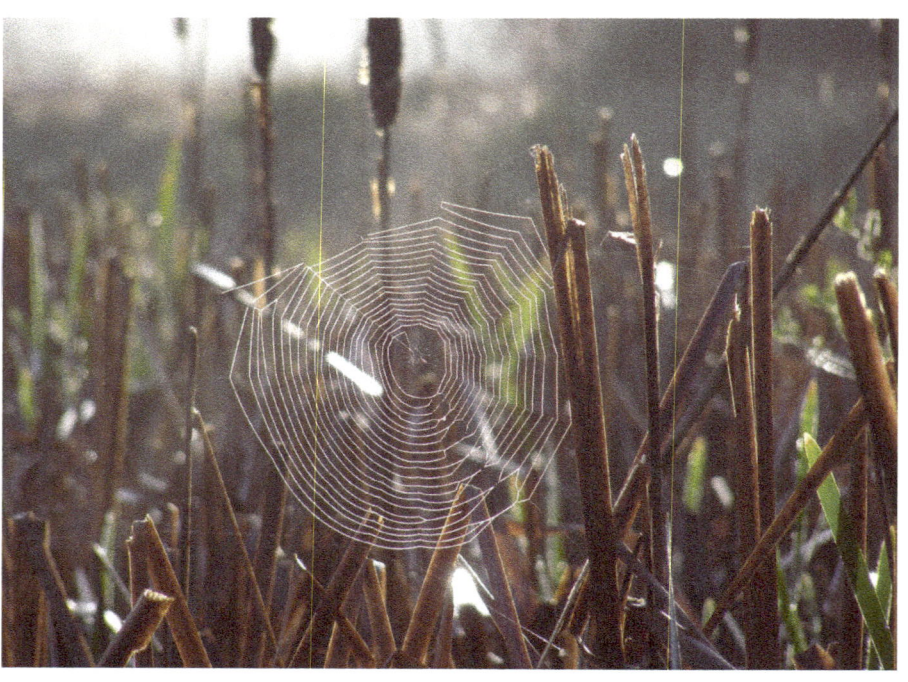

ORB WEB

This arachnid amidst autumn cattails
spins slow dreams of no-see-ums
for hors d'oeuvres, flies for entrée,
abdomen of ant for light dessert.

He shoots out thin bridge-lines
before coarser filaments flow
from spinneret, take hold, begin
to circle like irregular sound waves.

He's no perfectionist, but the job
gets done. After labors he'll rest
in the eye of his web with no need
for camouflage, his colorless body
hidden in the hub of his creation,
spoke legs blending with silk strands.

Eight eyes shut, he'll feel for more
than a breeze, jet to kill when tips
of legs sense a tug, hairs of taste
and sound vibrate through feet.

He'll cannibalize neighbors next door,
suck up meaty passersby unlucky in flight
with poisonous bite. He'll liquefy
their bodies for gourmet mash.

He'll fatten with pride of the hunt.

But first he must be patient and still
as the empty shell of a trapped insect
until the sparkling net of sticky dew
dries invisible and the sun disappears
behind thick cloud like the shut
eye of a camera capped and encased.

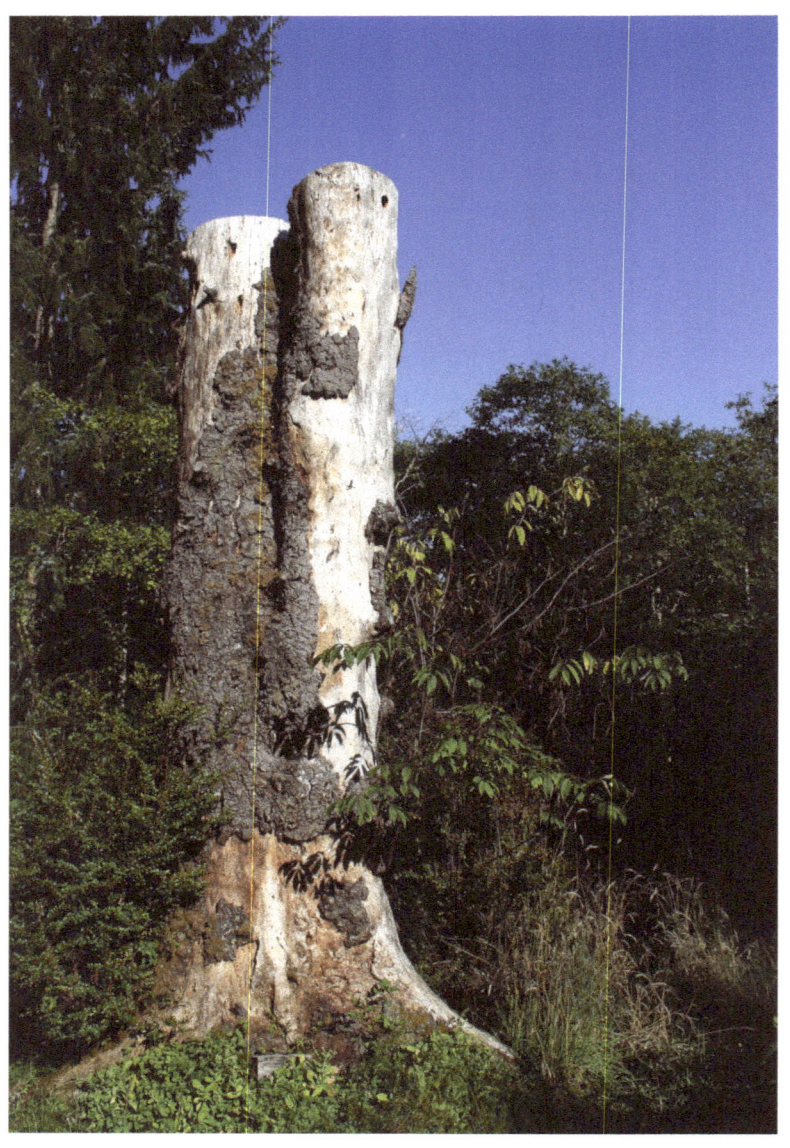

BAY VIEW SPRUCE

There's good reason for the young
spruce outside my study window
to lose heart like willows
in late autumn paling over dry
river banks. Their grandfather's
double-leader trunk amputated;
his shredded coat horny scales;
holes pecked in his pallid skin
by yellowhammers. Inner bark
once the only hope for near-life.

CLUMP OF SEAWEED ON THE LONGEST BEACH IN THE WORLD

How desperate you must feel
when anchors break free
from holdfast and dislodge you
from your saltwater dwelling.
Imagined wrack coursing through
your yellow veins; warty skin
like a toad or prickly pear
beginning to dry; bubble
cisterns emptying to quench
the never-ending thirst of sands.

Inconsolable as it might be,
know that your life lost makes
for new life found. Because
of you dull sands become jeweled
with glistening orange, trapped
waters become scales of threaded
mica, tidal streamlets become
miniature canyons. The world
stays fresh by disrupting familiar
places, shifting points of view.

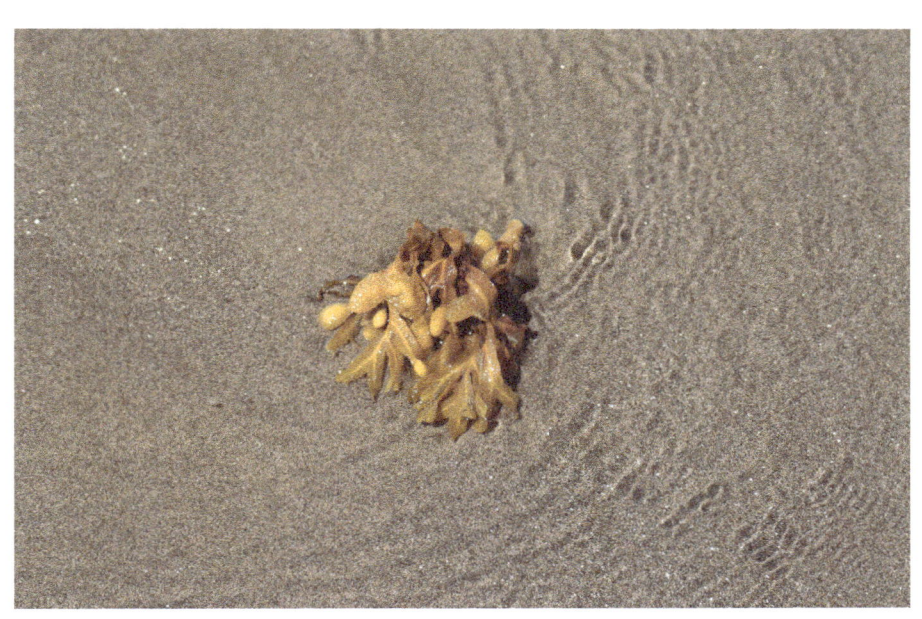

READING A SAND DOLLAR

Legends can bend the truth,
trick the eye, seduce the heart,
tie the mind in a bowline knot.
In this finely stitched
embroidered shell I see no life
of Christ as Easter lily
or magnet star, no nail or
spear holes agape in flesh
given way to bone, no white
dove bursting from heaven
or hovering in azure skies
to sing of a risen body.

If one's eye sees an insect,
make it a winged one at rest,
no butterfly burdened with symbol.
Better, see a common urchin
that bathes in shallow waters,
hides in Oregon sands grainy
as its self. See its live body
protected by filaments
as a thing securely matched
with place. And when its body
breaks like a mandala, watch
it give itself to living seas.

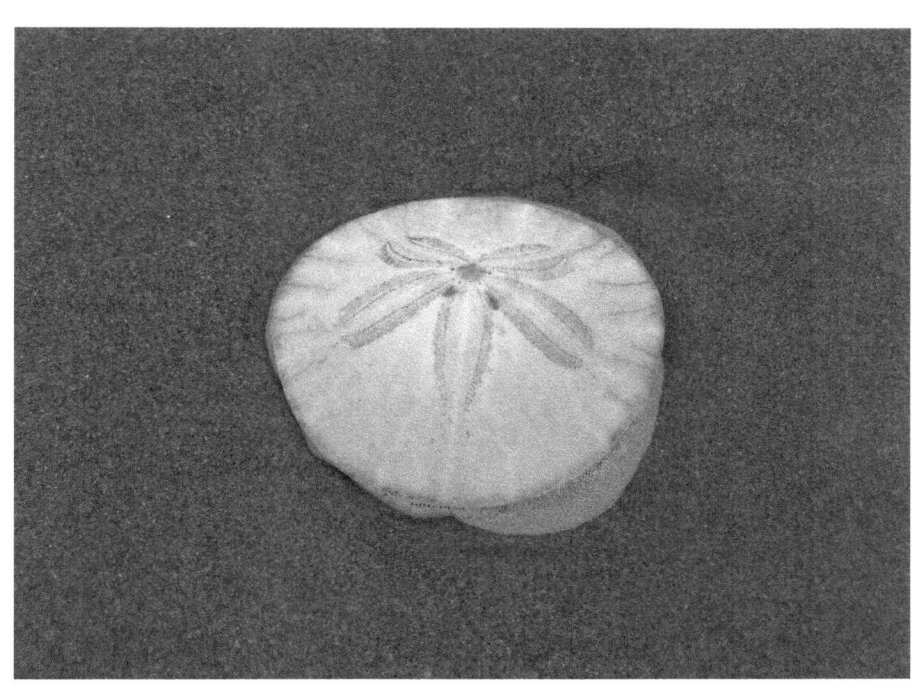

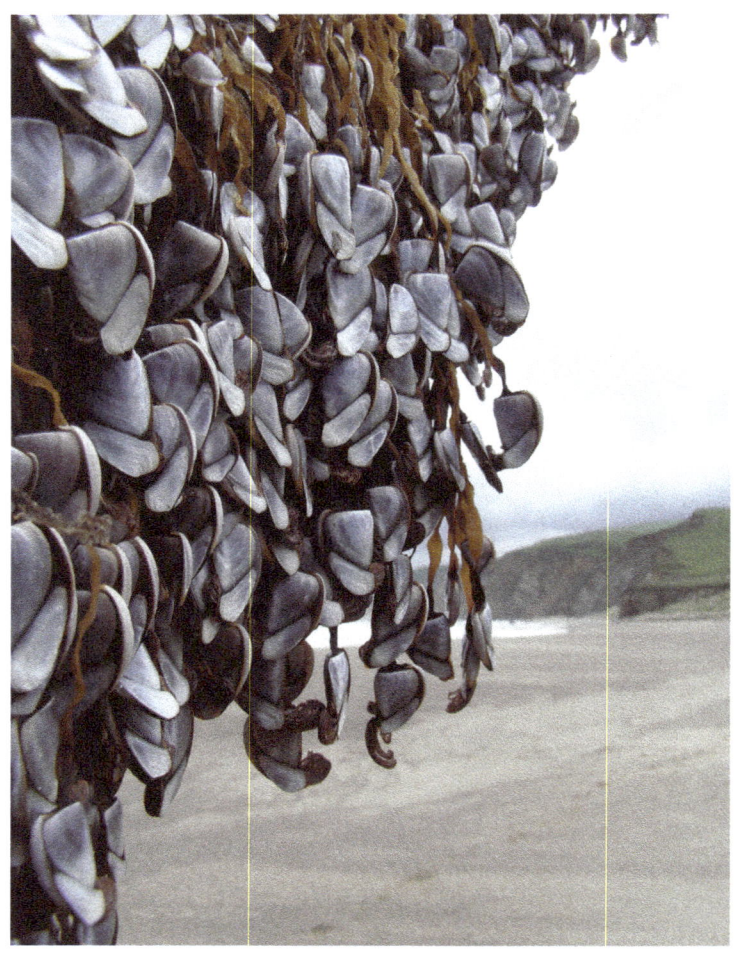

HANGING SHELLS NEAR KEHOE BEACH

Boneless lepas cling
for life to weeds of the sea,
metallic shells ring
calcareous melodies
like wind chimes in fragrant air.

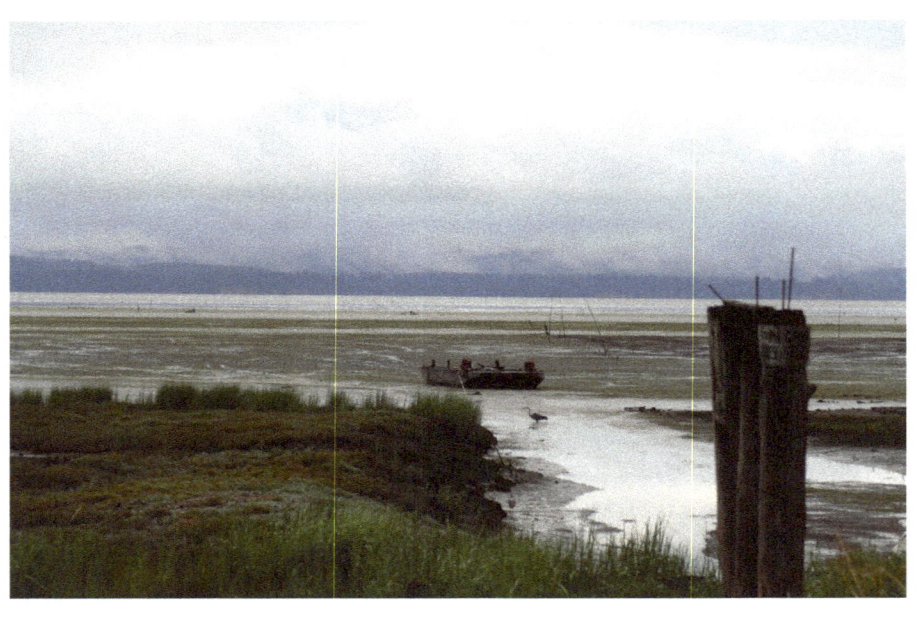

PICTURE WINDOW VIEW

First light pokes sluggish day,
Mudflats stretch like the sky.

Spiked tufts of eel grass sway,
Pilings defy decay.

A light wind nuzzles dock awry,
Blue heron breakfasts in the bay.

Earth returns again for me.

MORRO BAY

When dawn turns this great black
rock to seaweed green and brown,
three candlestick smoke stacks
of the defunct power plant cease
to blink red at it, otter pups wake
to play, gulls fill the sheltered
estuary with cries and coos, light
breezes ruffle poppy petals, rains
glaze toyon leaves India green
and bay shifts in its own way,
ebb from night and flow to day.

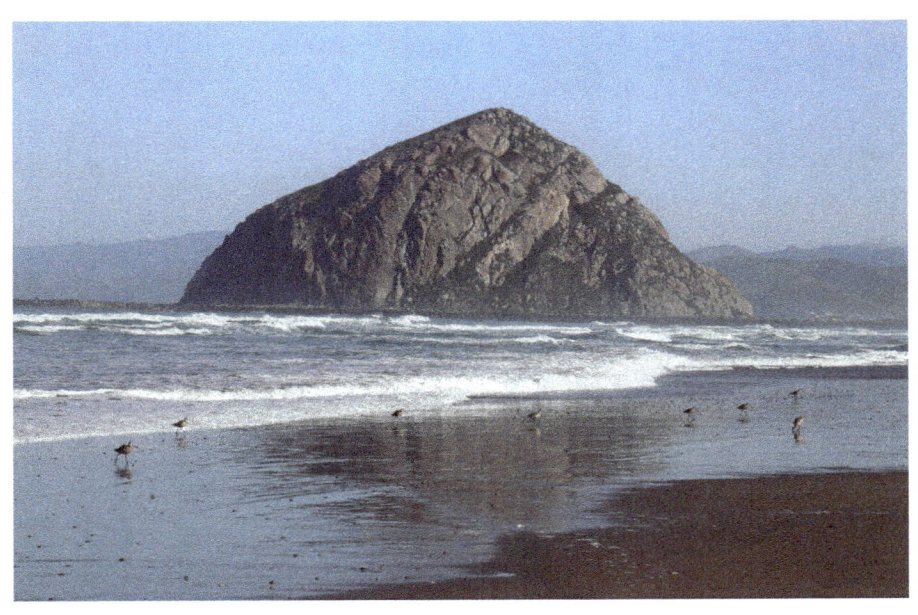

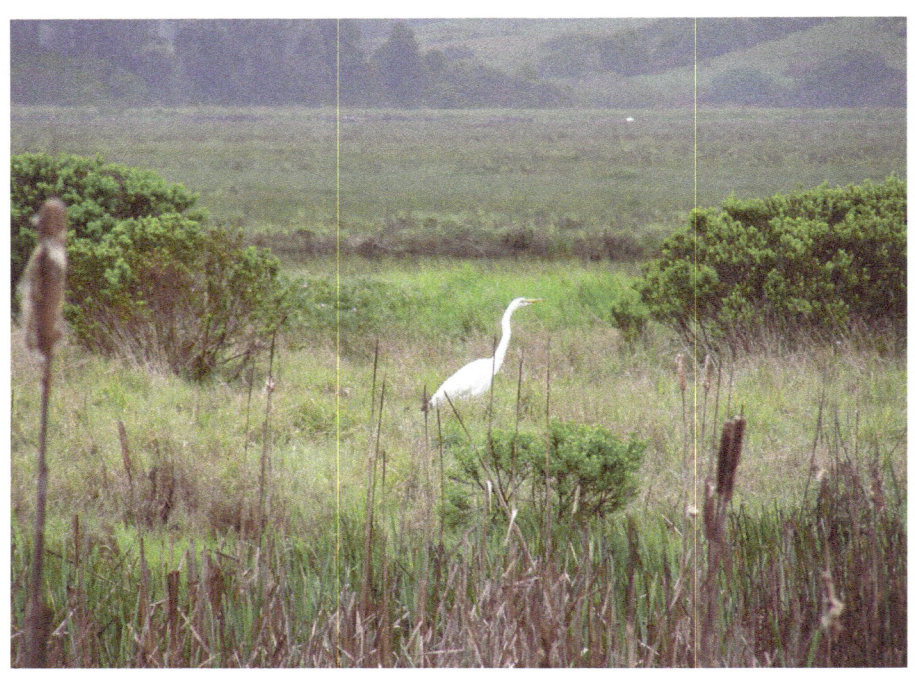

WINTER OUT THE BACK OF MARSH COTTAGE

Bolinas hills like green pillows rest on the bed of the bay.
Green haystacks of coyote bush dot marsh banks.
Clumps of bamboo in green feathers stand tall.
Iris leaves point green daggers toward spring.

Only cattails crack under the season,
lose furry tips, break down
into splintered sticks of blanched beige,
as if stubble in a corn field.

But, too, only cattails feel the brush of luminous egrets
slow-step by them with measured elegance,
hear marsh wrens
fill barren flutes with radiant green trill.

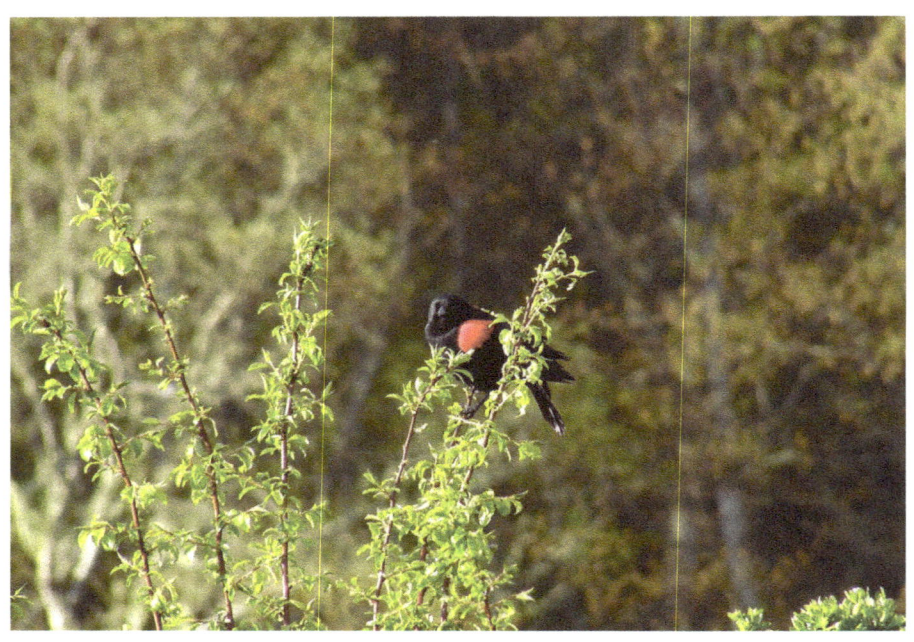

ROMANCING ON TOMALES BAY

This red-winged black bird
in the heat of spring
sings his blood song
against tawny marshland,
gray mist, pale woodlands,
flits from stalk to stalk
in seductive salsa steps,
flashes his red chevron
like a bachelor general
in ballroom quest of a princess.

Beneath his glistening black coat
heart skips beats, body trembles.

SNOWY PLOVER

Tiny puff seed pod
how you blend into white
surf, gray beach, brown dunes,
scurry like a wind-up toy
against extinction, mother
cotton balls on toothpicks
to preserve your race.

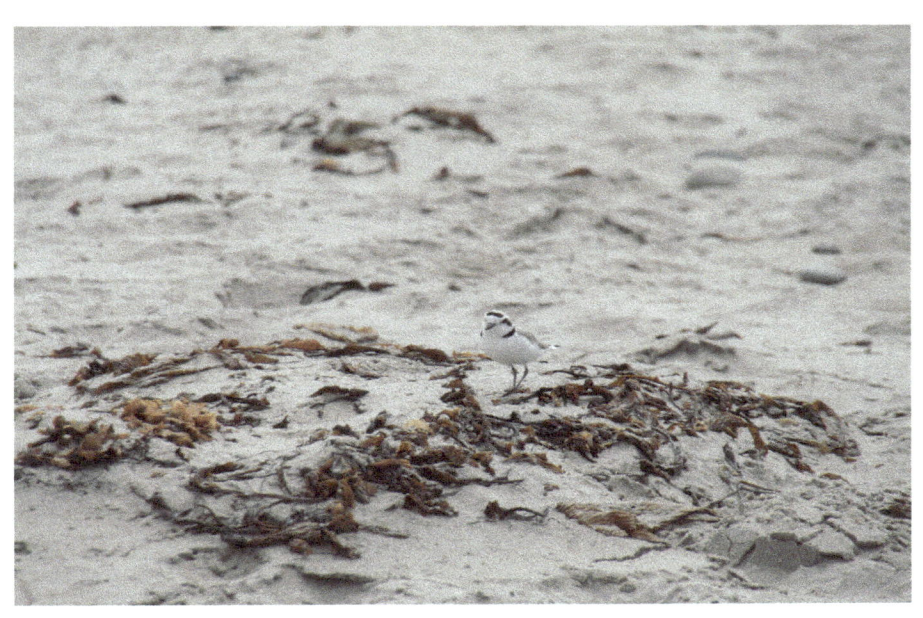

IN DEFENSE OF DEVIL'S IVY

Why, tame Solomon Islander,
do they call you devil's ivy,

you without bat wings, dragon
scales, horns, cloven feet?

You're no red-faced solipsist,
your green stems winding upward

and downward in easy, sure steps
like angels on Jacob's ladder.

You delight in variegation,
leaves waxed viridian and cream.

You a bouquet of shapely hearts
snug in shade, tinged with light,

blessed with beads of droplets,
seraphic tears of joy.

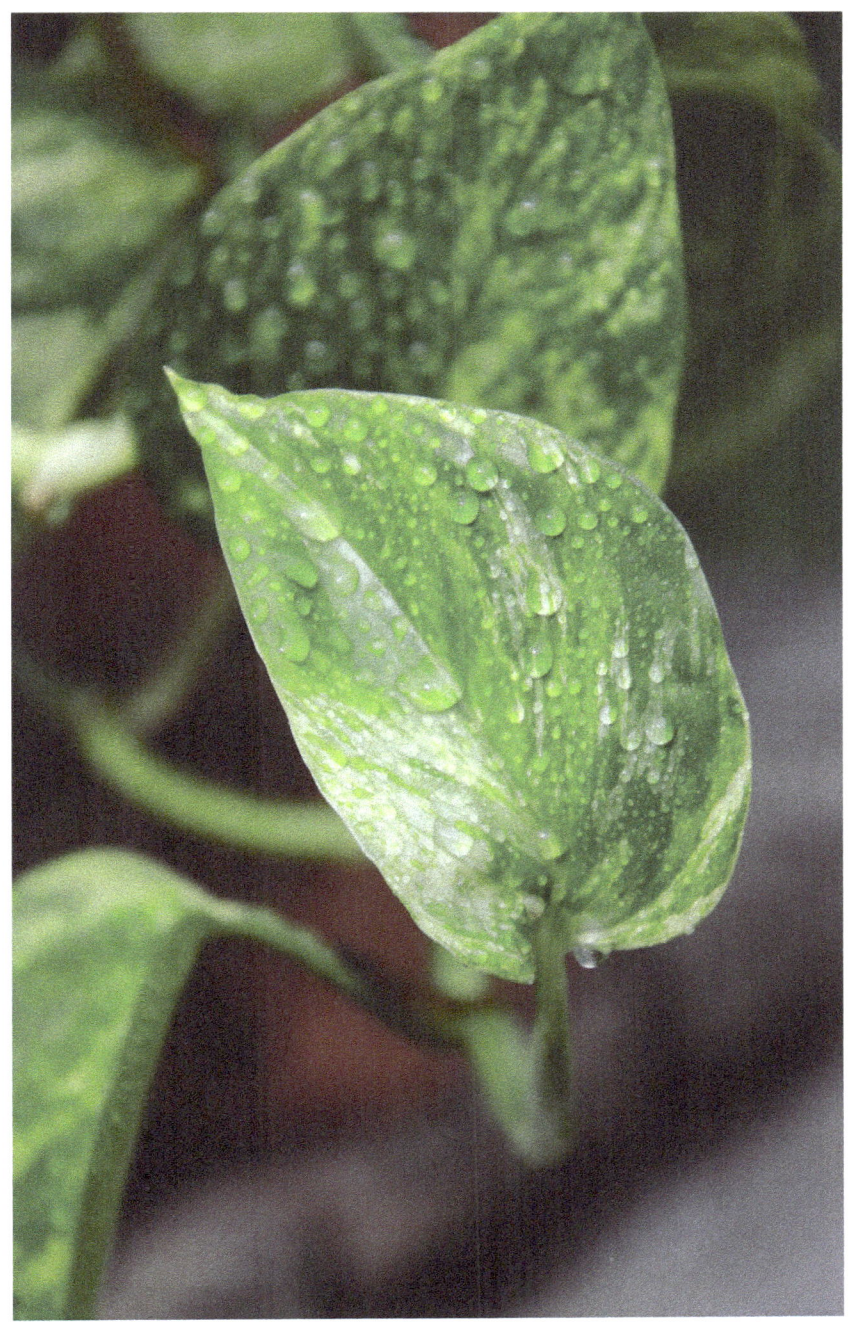

WHITE HIBISCUS

Coarse cotton
in embryo

blast of wool
with birth

folds of linen
to bless.

Something new about a flour.

Bright white
Shots
Blossid in
color/strucn

He really liked it
Blast in the center.
loves the shading and grey
shadow it self the

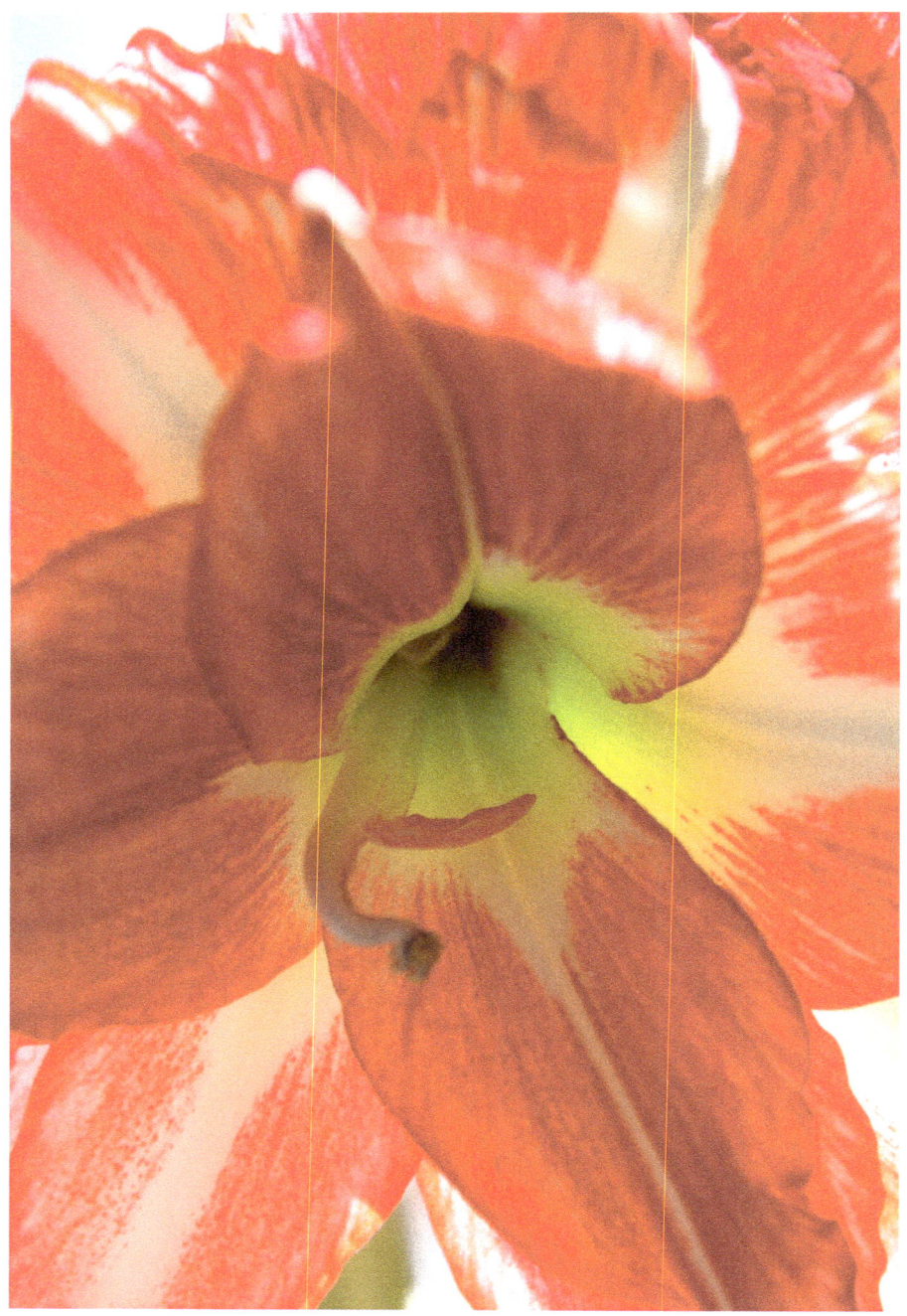

AMARYLLIS

shoots up stiff as a pole,
head poised to split open
and birth triplets or more.

Part sounding rod, part lover
trumpeting newfound beauty
with welcoming breaths.

Male and female together,
equal as two, as one.

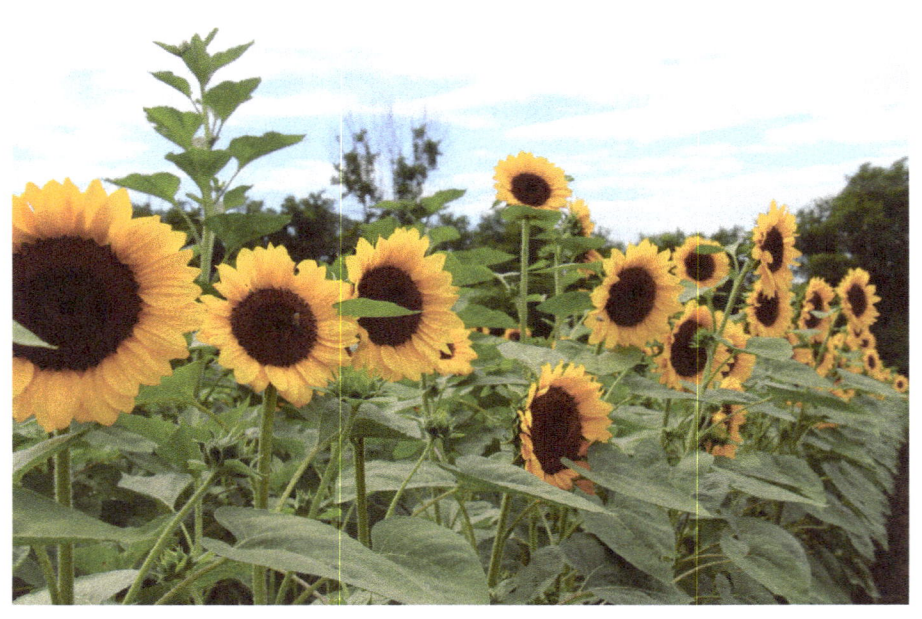

SUNFLOWERS

spring from tawny weeds,
    bristle with fine hairs
        fanned by broad leaves,

form buds wrapped tightly
    as cloth buttons by sepals
        for flowers to unfold,

beget tentacles that swim
    in the gentle current
        of summer's breeze.

There they bathe
    in the watery eye of day
        until filaments drown

in streams of petals
    bursting like fountains
        to celebrate

showers of seeds
    cascading like honey
        from golden combs.

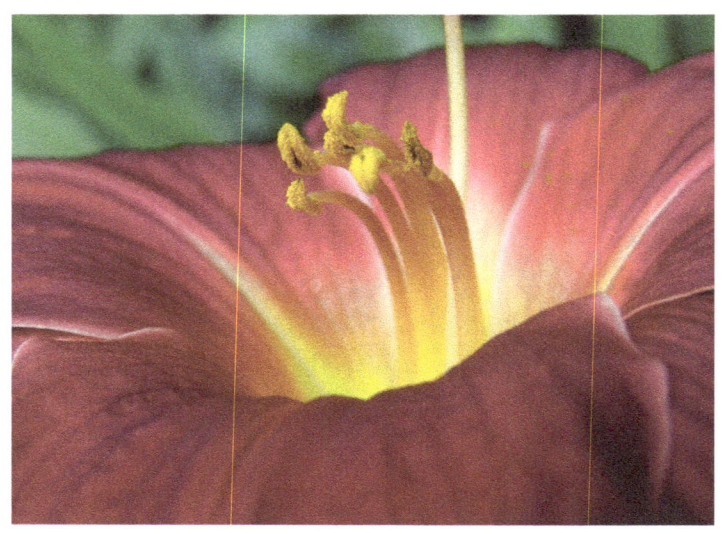

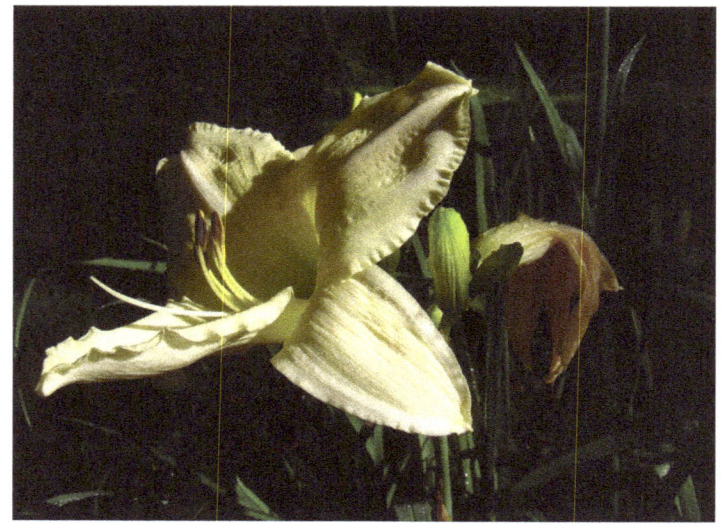

TWO DAYLILIES

At the height of day
corona radiata,
tongues crowned with nuggets.

At day's last light—bud,
bloom, crepe petals, spent blossom.
Shadows, shade, blackout.

THE SMELL OF FLOWERS AND WOOD
—for Bruce

Like a pollinating bee, my artist friend bobs and weaves
to find for his paintings the most fragrant flowers.
Lilacs in his dooryard, cascades of wisteria, lily
of the valley carpets, heady clusters of hyacinth.
Why he snubs wood I do not know. To cure him of this nasal
bias I'll recommend a few sniffs of rift-sawn white oak
or saw-milled spruce and tell him it's honey to run
his nose along a sticky limb of dripping pine. If that
doesn't convince, I'll pull my aromatic clincher—
hickory for his potbelly stove to clear his noggin
of tar-thick oil and turpentine in his malodorous studio.

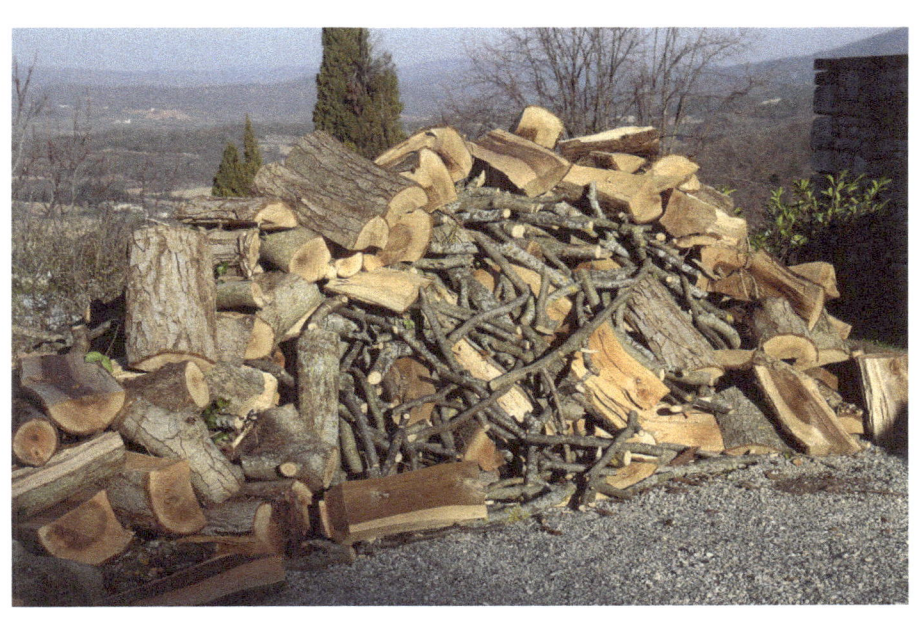

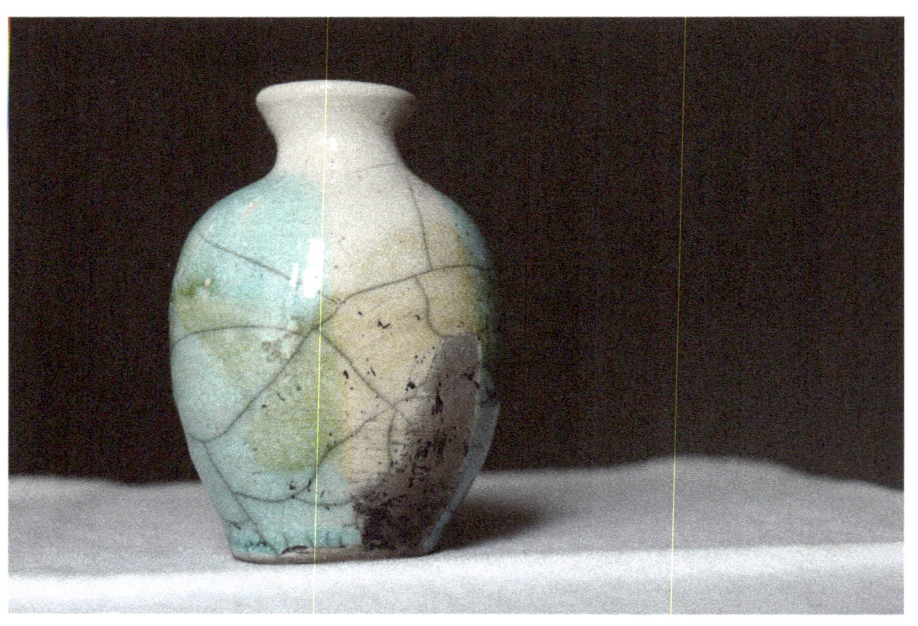

RAKU VASE
—for Nancy

This artifact is filled with a past
it does not know yet repeats,
full of a present it feels
but cannot know, vaguely aware
of a hopeful future it can share.
It's an earthy child of fiery accident
shaped by good and bad fortune pulled
to birth by iron tongs, sprinkled
with sawdust before scrubbed clean
of ash. Its unglazed black surface
registers soft gray, scattered,
unknowable ideograms. Its two glazed
surfaces a clouded sky and aqua sea,
its finish scarred with irregular,
unintended cracks no two the same.
It stands on a rough base out-of-round
with small mouth open wide to welcome
a cluster of short-lived wild flowers.

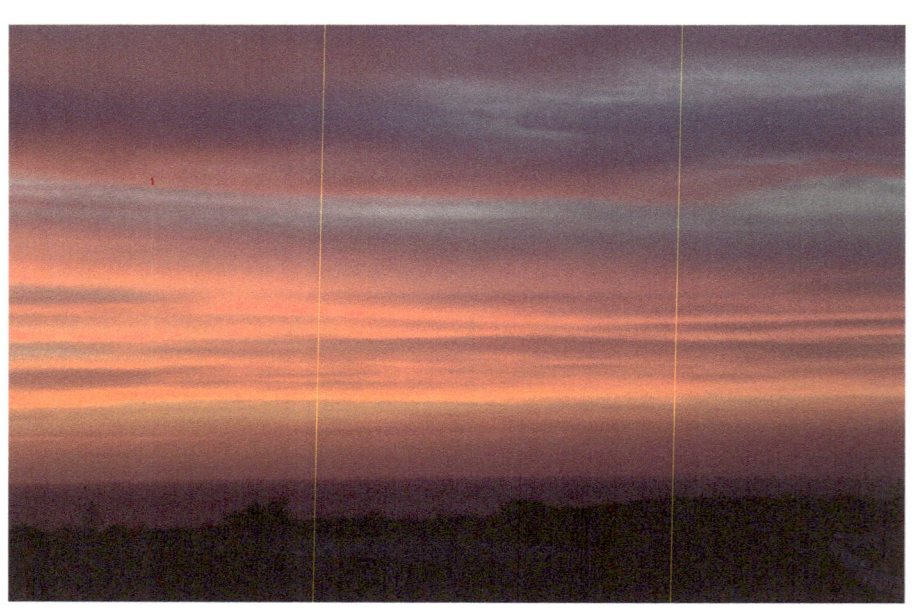

DIURNAL

Vault of night gives way
to sanguine sky, blackened land,
hope and dejection.

LAKE AT DUSK
—after Wang Wei's "Deer Park"

Spacious mountains shelter campsites,
echo words but no one seen.
Last light of day enters the forest,
mosses shine resplendent green.

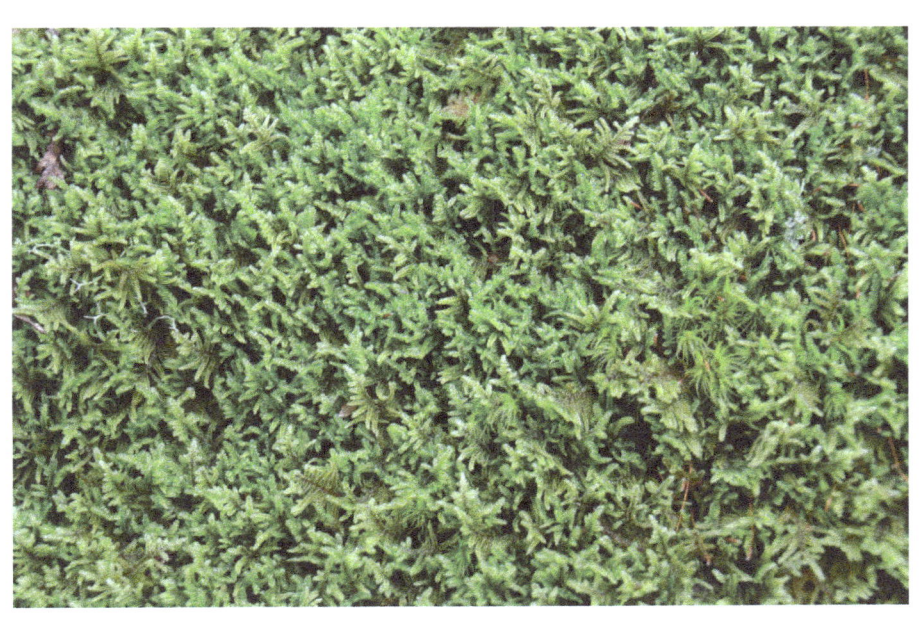

LAKE AT DAWN

First light of day
    blankets darkness,
mountains swell
    capped with clouds.

Silhouette of trees
    marks night's passing,
shimmering lake
    tinged shimmering pink.

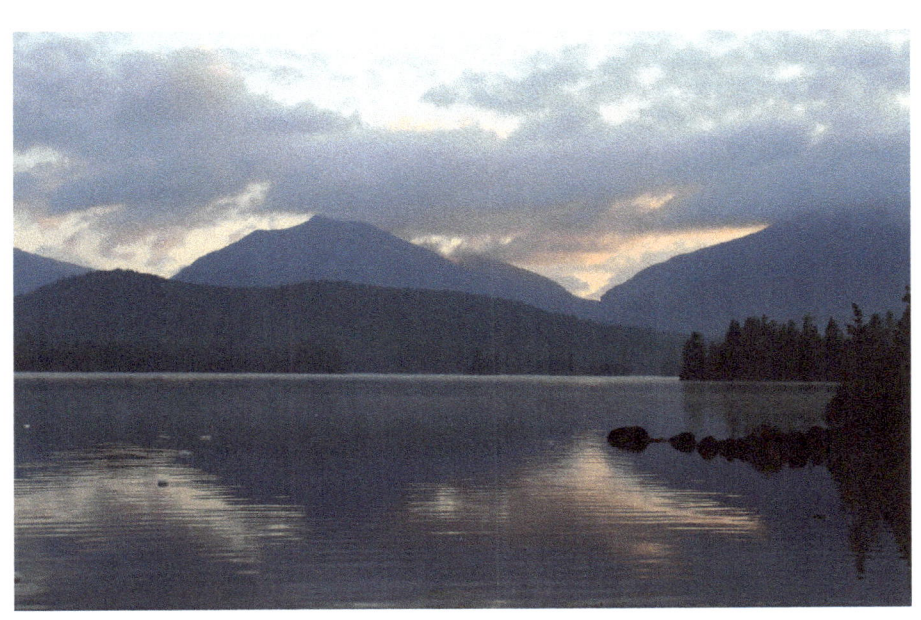

EAST

NAMES AND PLACES 1984

"Schenectady," an old friend
from the far west with yet
a passion for origins asked,
"Where does it come from? What
does it mean?" All I knew
for sure was that it's Algonquin.
But it isn't. It's thought to be
Iroquoian, "Scag-nac-ta-de,"
"beyond the pine plains." Or,
for a curious shift to metaphor,
it could be "S'quan-hac-ta-de,"
"beside the open door."

East from my back door plain
on plain of pines once spread
like Persian carpets—tall,
straight backed, with the smell
of pitch, scrape of needles,
spongy beds. Woodlands cleared
by Shakers for farm land, cabin
beams, window frames, winter
fires. Today tarmac runs
beside their meeting house,
jets scream like speared horses
above their burial ground.

—continued

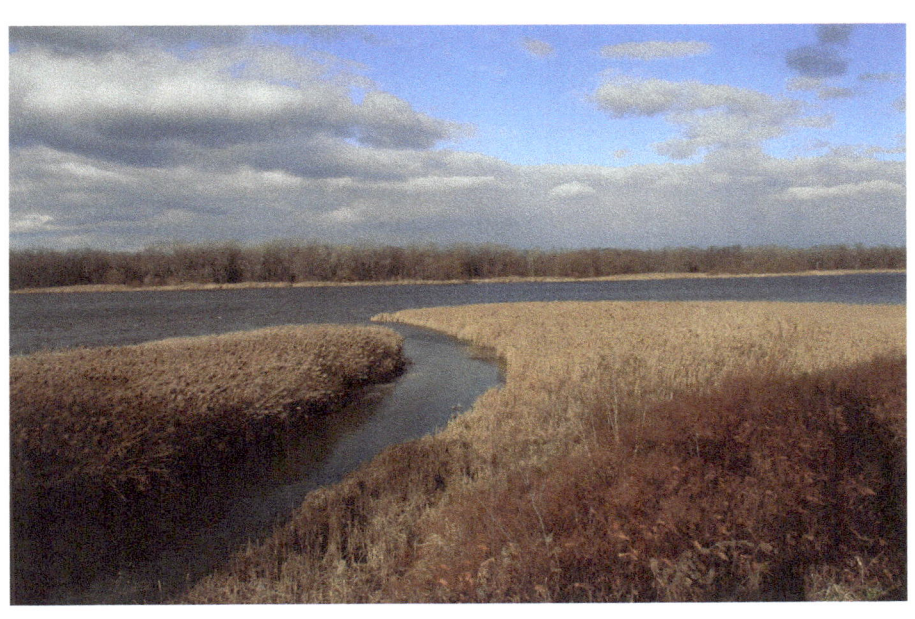

West from my front door toward
that door still open to the Mohawk
Valley macadam winter-pocked
and torn reveals underlying trolley
tracks from seventy years ago.
Today the electric city barely
lit: eyeless street lamps, ashen
warehouses, vacant shops forced
to weather too many hard freezes
and unseasonable thaws. Too much
expansion and contraction for
warm-blooded immigrants to bear.

At times I'd like to close this door
but can't. For here I'll work
a working life, talk shopkeepers
into friends, learn to care
with wife and children about local
places, people, names. After it bends
around Schenectady like a snake
in search of its tail to mouth
the Mohawk river tends easterly,
turns its back on my inquisitive
old friend and his newer, open,
simpler side of our land.

SKUNK CABBAGE IN OUR WETLANDS

Mercy, you do stink!
Worse than any skunk
terrified to be a fur
doormat with tire tracks.
Your blossoms burn nose
hairs, your torn leaves
tear eyes. Stoneflies adore
your stench, take pride
in spreading pollen
from anther to stigma.

But olfaction and sleazy
breeding ground aside,
nothing can compete with you
when it comes to melting
ice, snow, swamps. You're
a thermogenic power plant,
a cornucopia of heat above
water with stem below pulled
deeper and deeper by roots
into luscious spring muck.

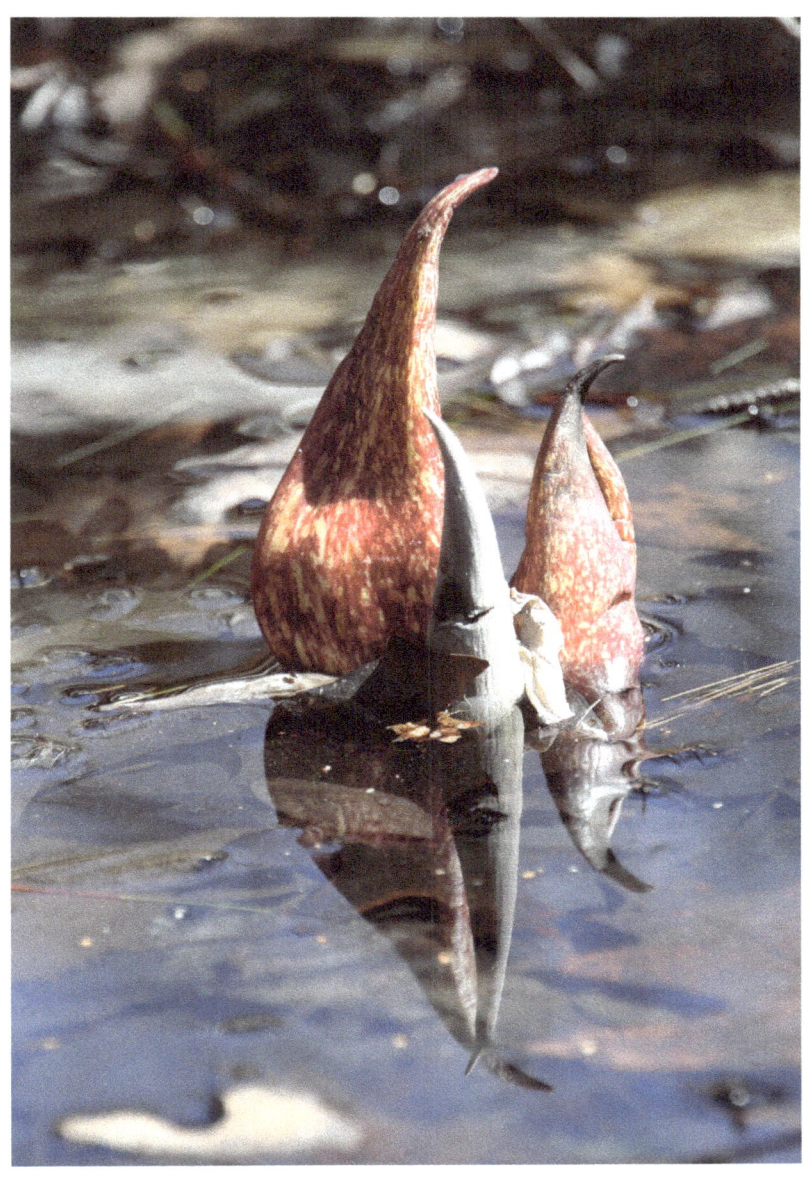

UPSTATE

Trillium in Swedish
translates as triplet, its
three leaves, three petals,

three sepals on rootstock
trilling to shake off spring
chill in wet woodlands.

It's a lily but no trout lily
with speckled leaves swimming
beneath bumblebee yellow stars.

It's as white as blood root
but flaunts no stamens
that burst like tiny flares.

Together this triptych to warm us
with candescent suns, salve
the bite of New England ice.

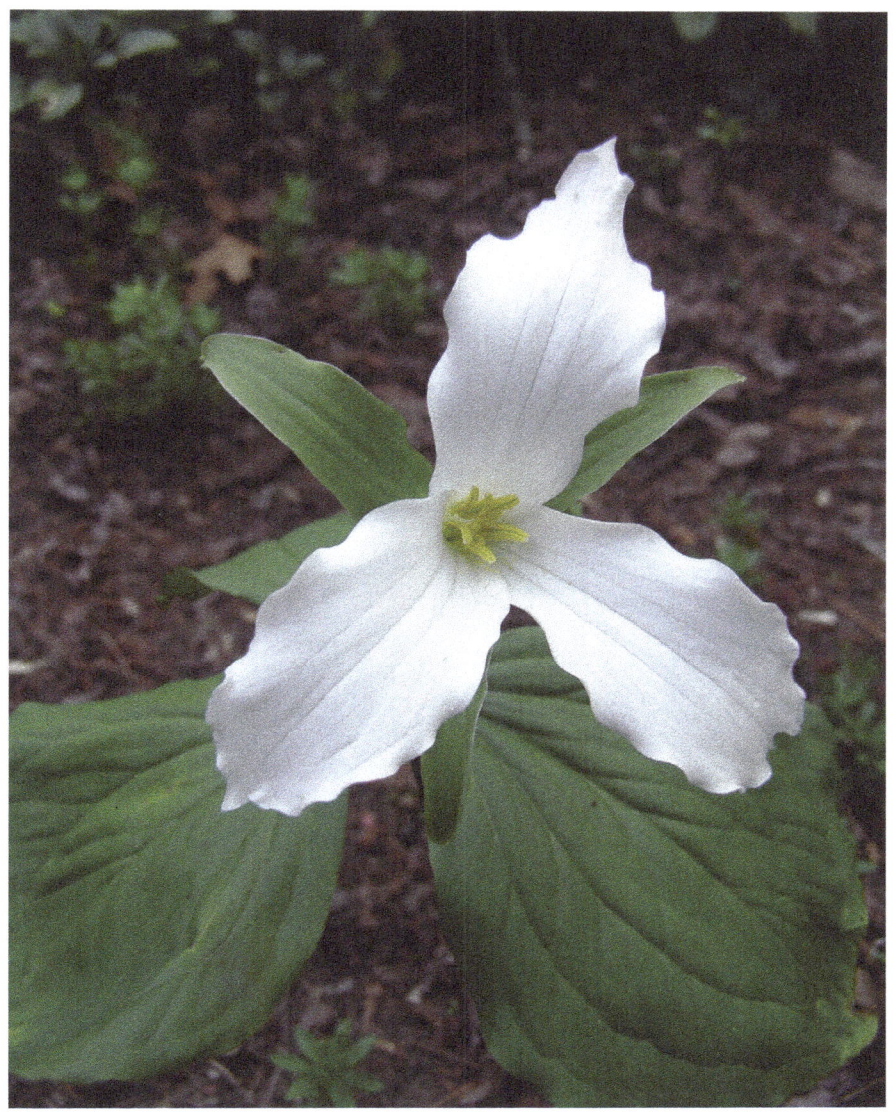

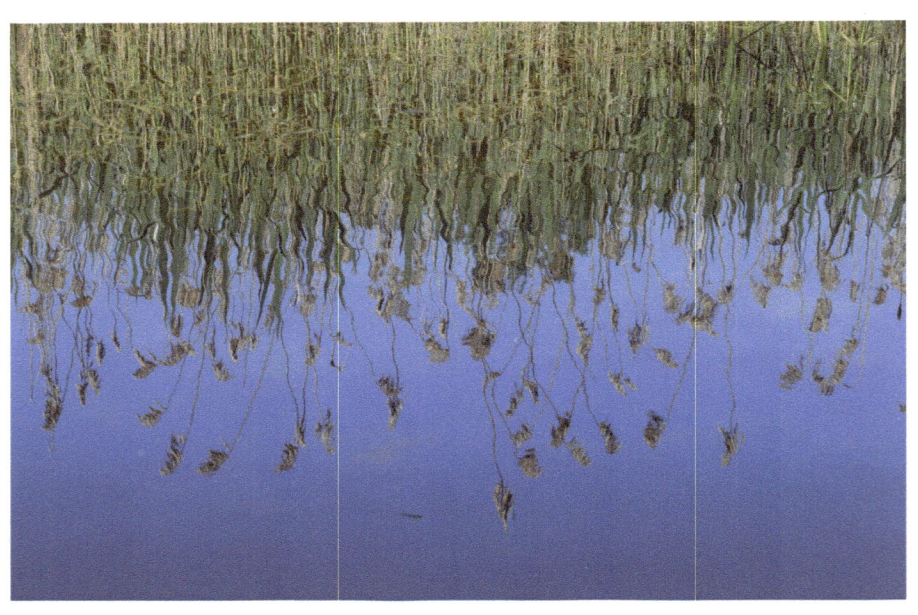

SPRING POND NEAR SARATOGA

What a life to feel changes in body every day.
Thunderstorms fill you up, suns dry you out.
Belly full and round one day, a basin of mud
the next. And there's no way for you to stay
at an even level. You could be dammed, you know,
which would be much worse. Thank Gaia you're able
to adjust, at times can even—like this photo—
turn strands of common reeds into ringlets.

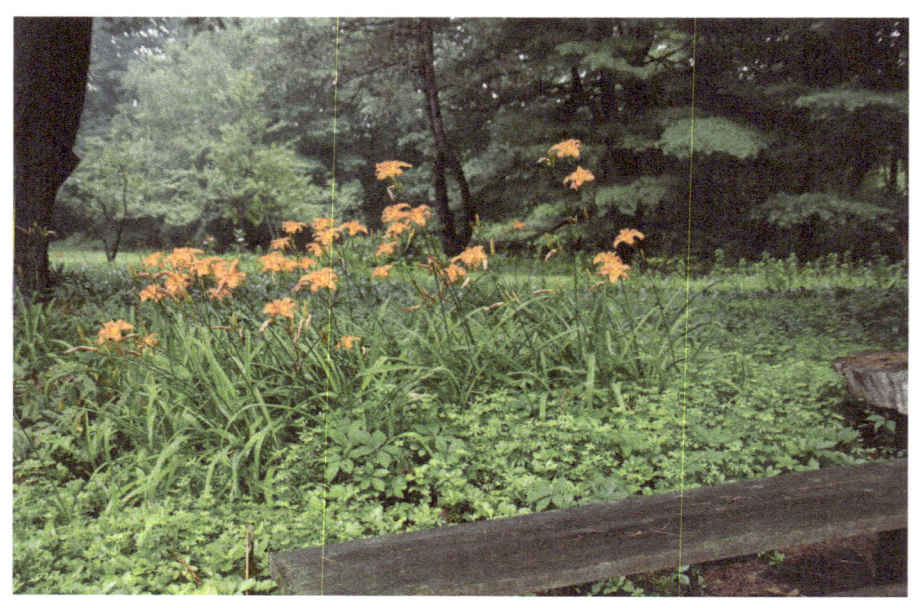

2.6 SUBURBAN ACRES

Let others cultivate their lands
ordered and tidy as English gardens,
well-plotted as Cumbrian hedge rows,
harmonious as the heavenly spheres.
We want ours to appear wild,
without muzzle, bear its teeth
to symmetry through all seasons.
Want it to roam free, sniff its way
from birthing light to nurturing shade
to deathly darkness as it pleases.
We hide pathways of grass and pine
needles so visitors lose their way.
We plant apple, cherry, peach, and pear
out of line to dizzy our white spruces
standing soldier-like in straight rows.
We leave andromeda and yew branches
untrimmed like tomatoes out-of-cage.
Our lilies of the valley and thyme
run rampant. Our clematis climb free
as runner beans, our forsythia blaze
splintered rays against all reason.
Our gravel driveway serves as crime
lab for crabgrass and dandelions.
Such delight in disorder is possible,
we know, because of the assured return
of spring daffodil, summer peony,
autumn chrysanthemum, winter holly.

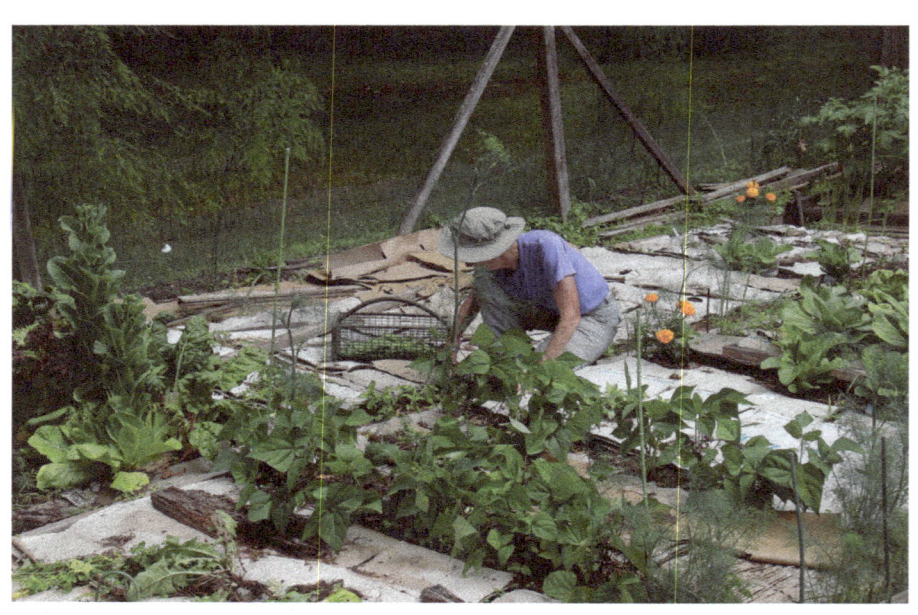

THE INDUSTRIOUS COTTAGER
   —for Carol

She just can't be still.

Lettuce, cucumbers, chard, carrots to plant
with crusted hands. Tomatoes and peppers
to support with unwieldy frames. Daylilies,
forsythia, turtleheads to shift from bed to bed.
Ferns to nurture and ferns to compost. Chives,
sage, oregano, basil babied before clipped
for table. Gloves by Womanswork to fetch kindling,
stack split maple. Deep digging for fruit trees
in memory of brother, mother, father. Less than
a toe print whatever she does, wherever she goes.
The payoff before dinner: a glass of wine
from Aveyron, roll of Sainte Maure de Touraine,
wedge of Roquefort, button of Picodon.

Every act with attention, care, grace.

ADVICE TO A PAINTER OF STILL LIFES

It's time for you to step outside your studio
to that other world of greens and browns,
grass and trees, plots and subplots where Adam
delved. Sketching gardens in pastel can loosen
a painter up, soften hard edges of framed beds.
There's no need for precise detail when you plough
ground, work your colored sticks like pitchforks
with twisted tines, turn over textured soil
to let fresh air in. Leave the lawn shaggy, unkempt
for another good lesson. Then put down your chalk,
kick shoes off, hop about like a speckled robin
just nudged out of nest and relish earth's wormy-ness.

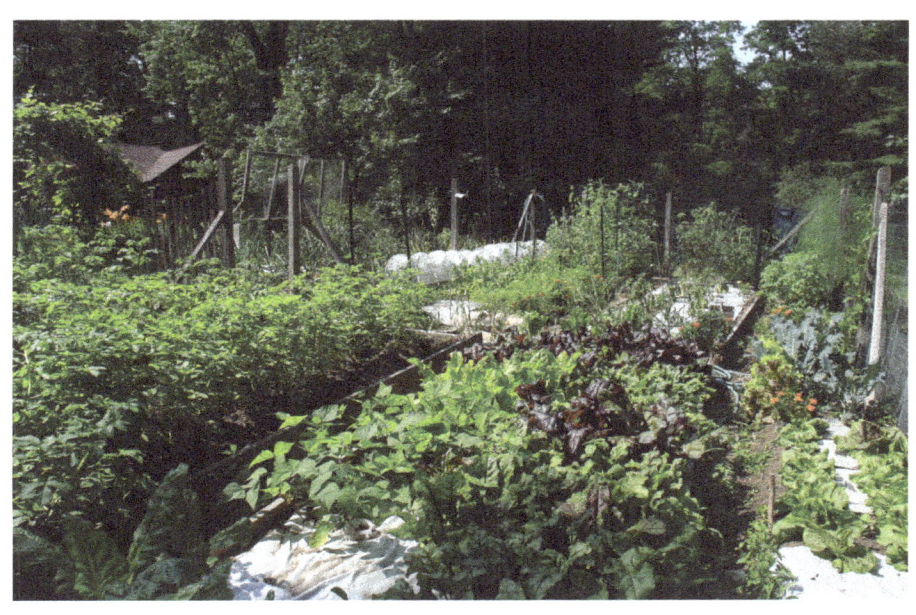

NATURAL HISTORY
*/ˌnaCH(ə)rəl ˈhist(ə)rē/ :The scientific study of animals or plants,
especially as concerned with observation rather than experiment . . .*
—Oxford English Dictionary

Though not as radiant red and orange
as cardinals, posture-perfect,
cock-sure robins whistle out winter
sweetly too. Love lyrics in warbled
phrases as welcome as March sun stir
bulbs, nudge green spears of narcissus.
Even seasoned bird watchers go soft to see
couples mate, he pecking like a jackhammer
to feed her, she the pleased receiver
in courtship, nesting, parenthood.

In our shaded, trellised grapevine
with tangles of untended tendrils
a young couple chose to nest. Waist high
they darted by for four days to build
their suburban home of twiggy exterior
and grassy interior insulated with mud
and leafy vines. Then the laying of eggs,
her warm clutch, shells broken by three
beaks with mouths agape and throats
aquiver for earthworms to slide down.

We watched them feather and strain necks
above the nest's lip, heard soft infant
tweets and squeaks. Two weeks later
the absence of sound, song, and counter
song. The nursery emptied of nestlings.
Kissed by a light breeze the heart-shaped,
tooth-edged leaves brushed the partially
hidden nest. Shortly after, a flash of red,
woody shoots in his beak, she at work for her
second brood in taller, denser honeysuckle.

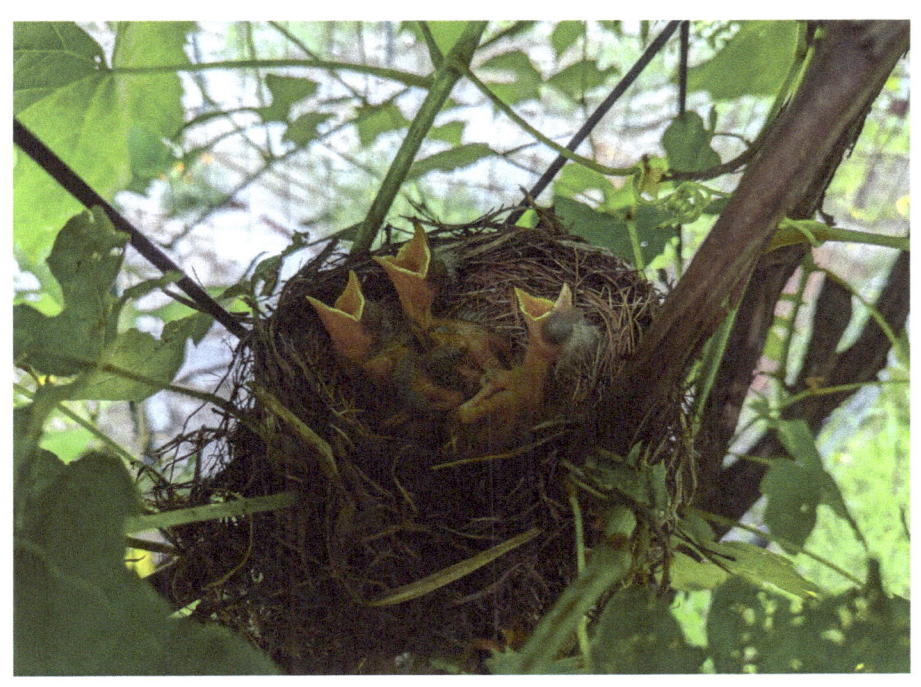

SERPENT IN OUR GARDEN

There's nothing sweet
about bittersweet. Don't
be taken in by its
unassuming flowers
or scarlet-orange fruit
tempting as an apple.
It strangles any tree
within its grasp,
a boa constrictor
who tightens with slow
intent to leave behind
a ghastly imprint
of its scales. It coils
unsubtle its serpentine way
around bark hard as oak,
soft as cottonwood, around
red spruce hopeful of light
and a full life. With
last gasp from the host
its leaves smile smug-green
at heavenly skies.

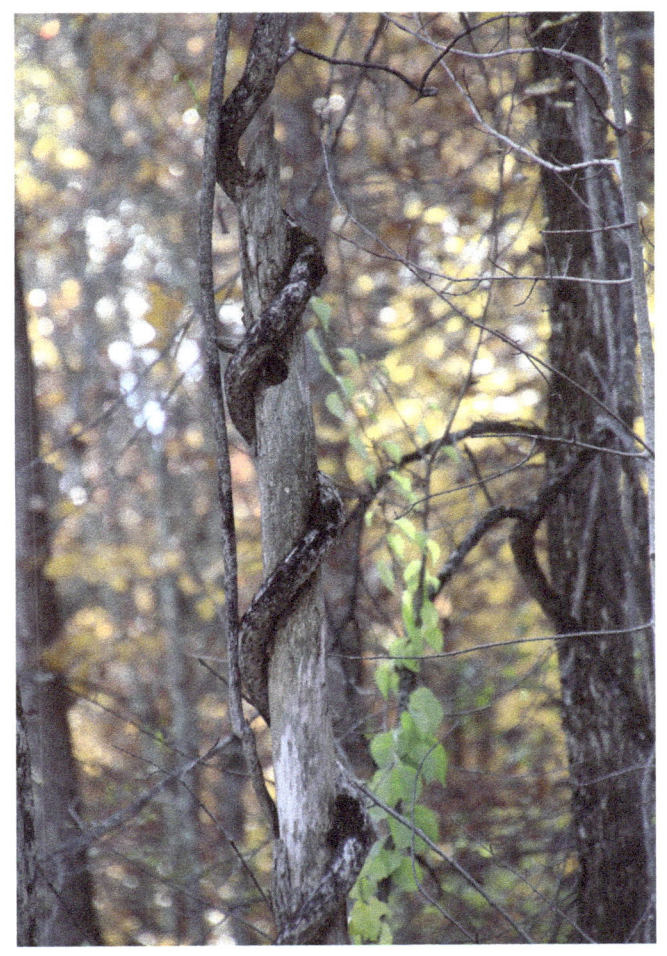

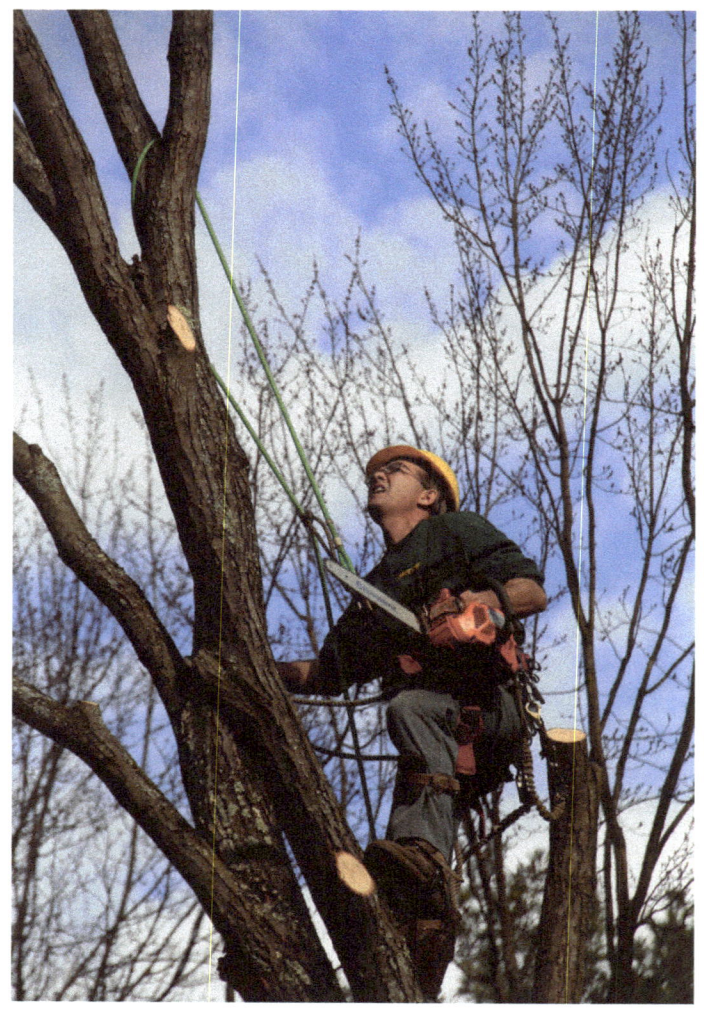

TREE HOPPER

The man's sturdy as a stump,
limber and strong as an oak branch
half way up an aged trunk.
He looks hard at our tree trimmed
with fungus, fidgets with clasps.
Chain saw and boot spikes glint
as he crawls like spider man
amidst the webs, like an old salt
who knows how much a spar can bear.
He tracks limbs, cuts them free,
slices branches as if butter, leaders
as if tenderloin till the tree
is reduced to a tabletop of rings.
He hops to ground, carves the trunk
into marble drums of a Greek column.

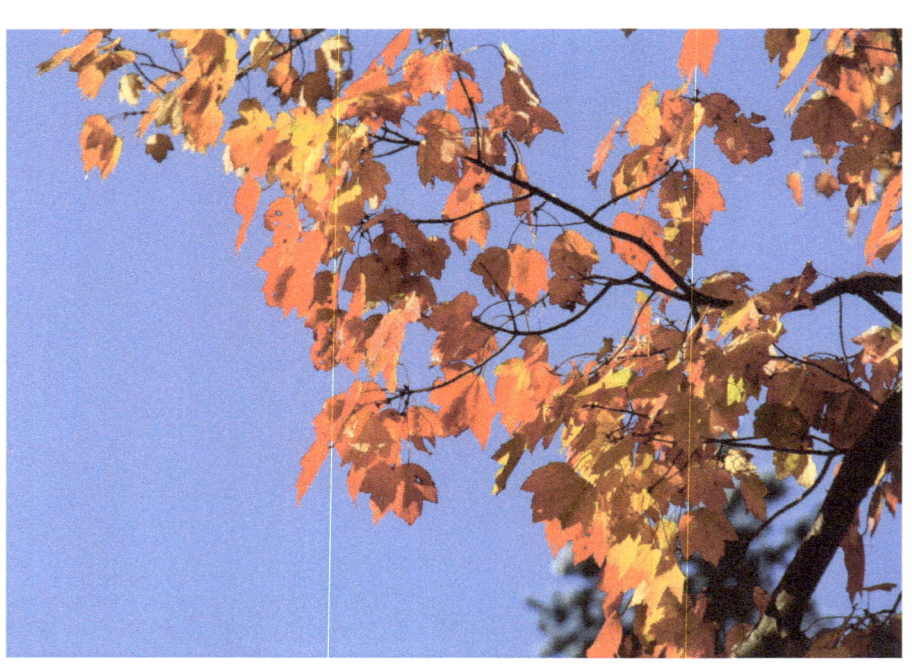

FELLED

Red maples at peak blind us
to diseased limbs and root rot.
When they cut this one to its stump
it flared like a Roman Candle, spun
like Catherine's Wheel, spouted
warm blood like a sperm whale
before its last, long, dying blast
of spray. "Most piteous," Melville
called the last. Pity then followed
by sighs of grief, heartful pain.

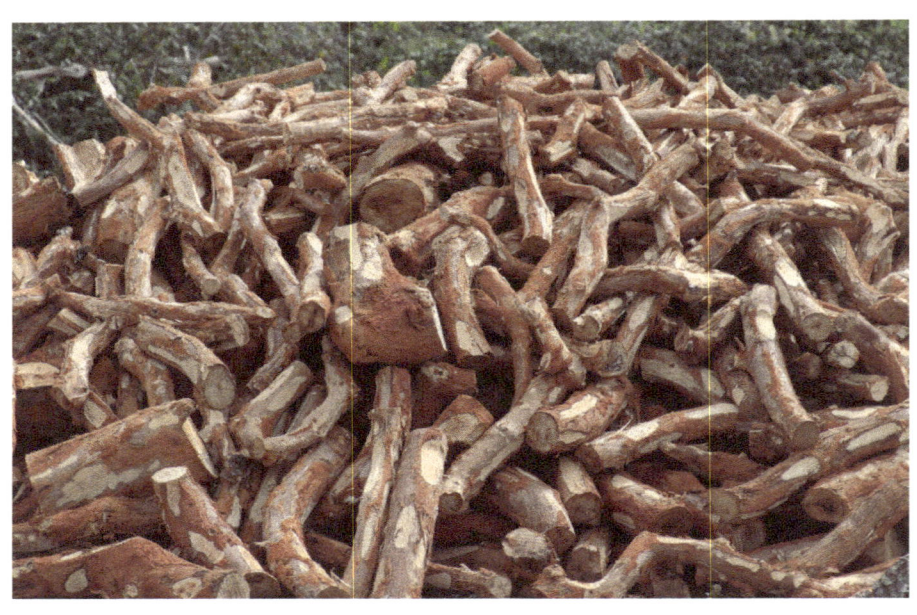

MERCY KILLING

I've always claimed that life
is for the living, to cut dying
wood from live trees no problem.
To my ear, groans and cries
from ailing boughs sapped
by too long life beg mercy.

This mildew summer of the slug
woodlands stood a jungle of apple
green to make anemic wood-spotting
easy. With conscience clear
I trimmed, cut, and chain sawed
maimed branches of pine and spruce,

maple and oak, to save them
from the indignity of suffering.
I told myself failed limbs
accept amputation, knowing
they'd soon be free of awkward
attachments to living trunks.

HADLEY MOUNTAIN FIRE WATCH LATE SUMMER

You're in your cab going
nowhere. Meter off. Eyes lased
on the forest for smoke coiling
thin as a thread snake or swelling
like a bonfire about to break
loose. Alone yet not lonely
in the company of boulders
washed clean with summer rain,
meadows of wildflowers, leafy
beech and birch bedded warmly
in loam. Woodlands for the moment
green spearheads dark as emerald
under the receding sun.

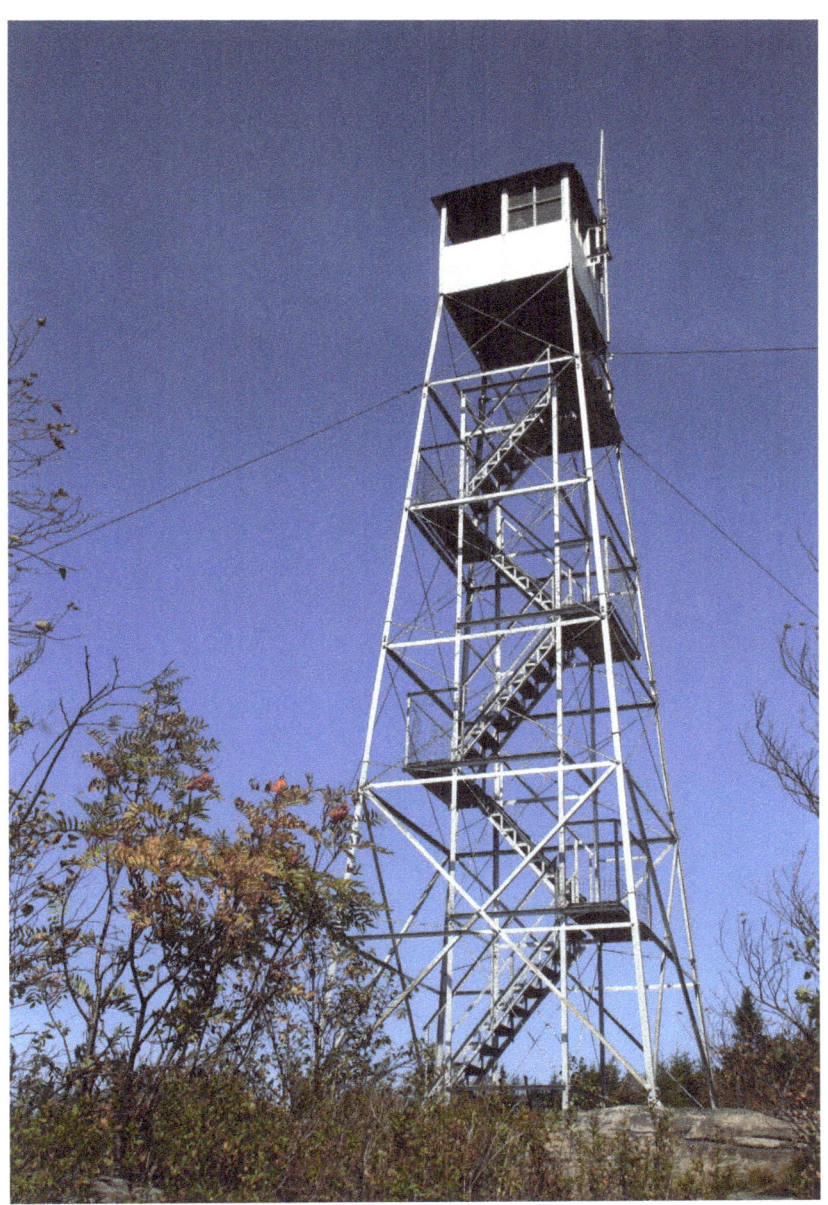

BLUE HERON

Some say the world will end
in silence pitch-black as night.
Some say in blasts of white.
I admit I'm drawn to light
and often wish to glide
unruffled as this heron
toward diamond-strewn waters
tinted celestial blue
with only a smudge of shadow.

But light can also blanch
what it touches, turn sparkling
waters into flecks of stubble,
dull luminous feathers, dissolve
delineation. Under this warping
light waters appear nothing
like the backdrop of black
at the Great Blue's back
studded with galaxies.

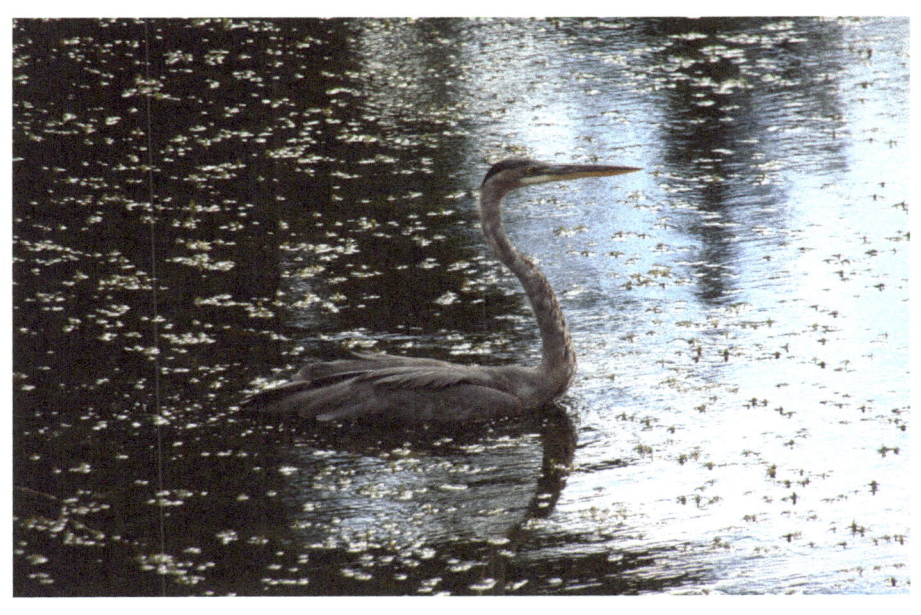

AUTUMN

Sugar maples brighten hillside palettes
to see us out of summer, turn anticipated
loss into momentary gain, then get us
to question gain, be suspicious of it.

After maples, restless tangles of color.
Red and russet oak shoulder lemon yellow
hickory, golden beech slip-knot
around evergreens that refuse chameleon.

White pines with sappy cones glisten
like spangles, shed sallow needles.
Magnolias strip naked to bony gray,
pale willows weep. Each leaf at the mercy

of the wind's sweet or bitter breath.
Leaves fated to float, drift, drop
like pollen with exhalations of fading light,
like snow with inhalations of night.

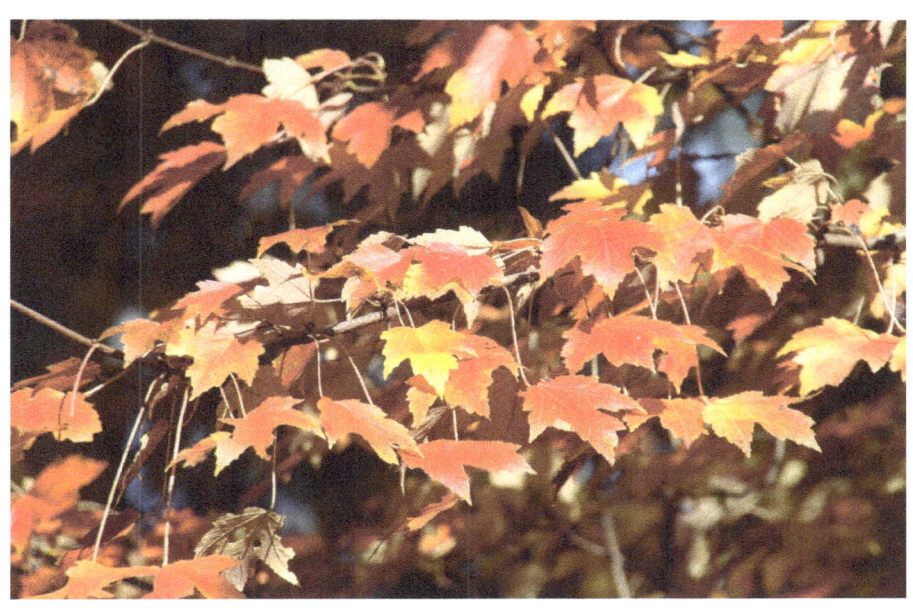

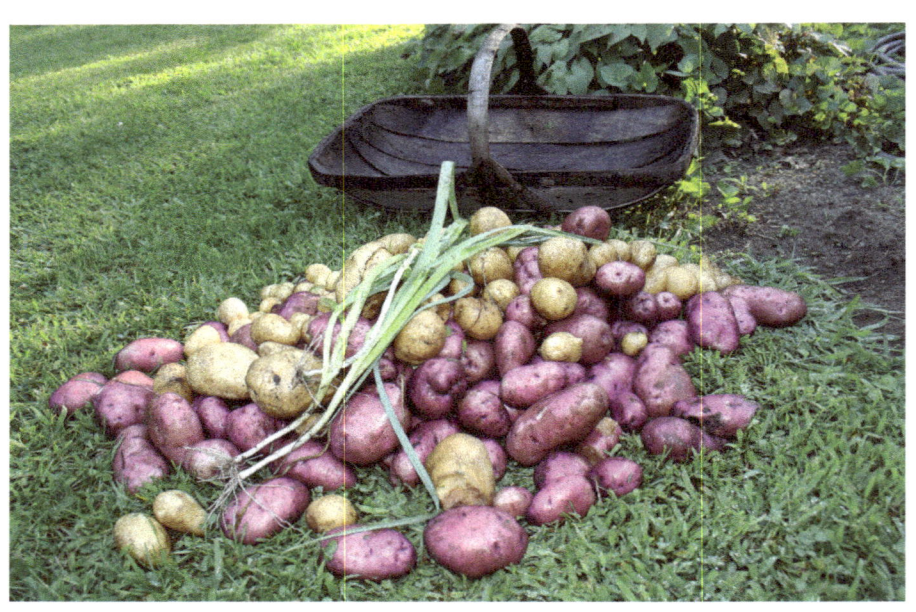

OCTOBER GARDENING

The day has come to accept gaunt yellows,
wan greens, wizened grays. Spent tendrils
of runner beans no longer with the energy
or will to climb tell us it's time to dress
like priestly philosophers and perform
a ritual where thoughts of past and future
planting, gathering, replanting meld
like birth, death, burial, resurrection.

We unearth potatoes, disentangle vines
that hide green tomatoes, tomatillos,
Lilliputian cucumbers. We check leeks
and kale for later harvests, plant garlic,
leave parsnip heads for aromatic April.
We flatten wire that protected sprouts,
rewind string that's not been pecked for nests,
straighten cages to cradle next year's crop.

For last rites compost comforters cover
every bed speckled with egg shells and
deliciously rich with pink worms eating,
laying eggs, defecating for spring beds.

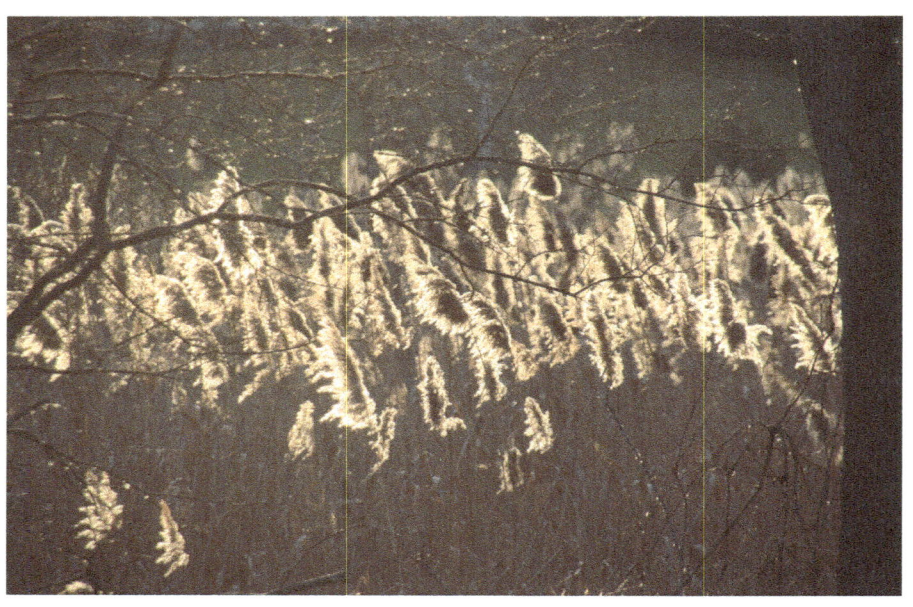

MIXED MUSIC

Sundown feathers autumn reeds.
A clutch of squirrels at supper eat
with teeth sharp as chef knives
the pumpkin we put out for grabs,
its orange face fated to blacken
and collapse into mush and dormant seed.
Peculiar how the grass they scamper
through looks greener these days than
midsummer green, the chokecherry
berries redder. Chipmunks underground
wrap regenerated tails about them,
doze before dark wintry sleep in beds
of tangled roots. Overhead, bare maple
branches cast nets to the unstable sky.

NEAR GIBBY'S DINER

Green fields sheared of hay
dotted with white marshmallows
bright as harvest moons.

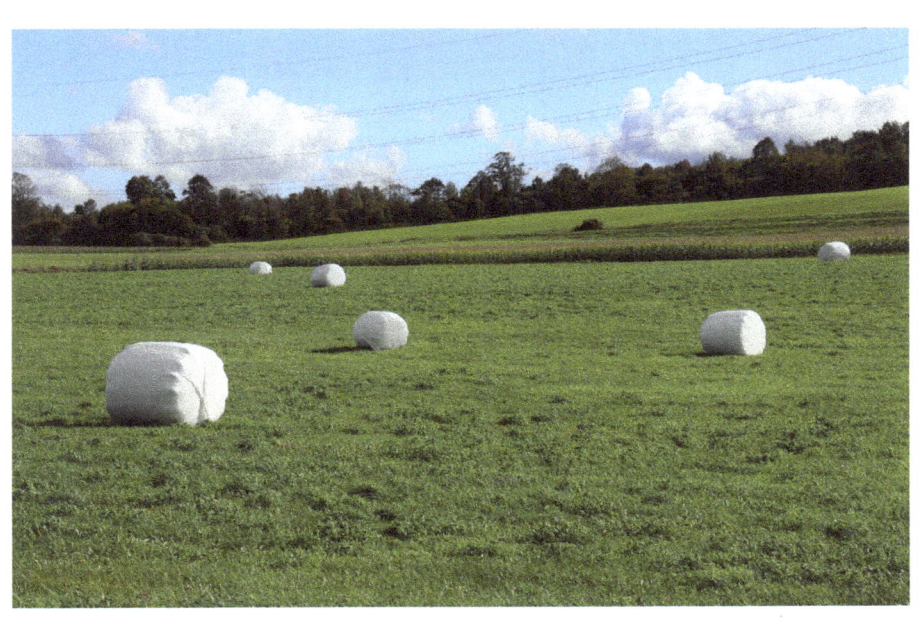

THANKSGIVING AT SALTSMAN'S HOTEL

"Fine country dining for over 200 years"
with still the feel of times from James
Madison to Teddy Roosevelt. When the stage
coach ran from Johnstown to Canajoharie,
horses got hitched to a post. When potholes
cratered roads and Model Ts kicked up
dust bowls, nights in the ballroom boomed,
the four small bedrooms held for hangovers.

Today we're greeted at the door by a little
lady in floral calico with polite smile
and four-course menu. Seating prohibited,
she says, until we order an entrée. Two
famous fried chickens we say, and we're on
our way past the stuffed skunk with tail
up and overstuffed raccoon dispensing
toothpicks in the bar where the backside
of mirrored Jack Daniels glows golden.

At our oil-clothed table: pineapple wedge
in cold slaw; bread pure white as a nun's
habit, airy and nutritious as cotton candy;
water pitcher large enough to quench
a hippo's thirst. Above us Robbie Burns
advertises his 10 cent cigar while courses
swarm like locusts till we become dirigibles.
Onion bloomers huge as giant peonies. Soup-
logged chicken chunks, rice, and Sunshine
Krispy Original Crackers tread broth, corn

fritters drown in sugar maple syrup. Fried
chicken crisp as pork crackling and juicy
as gossip at the next table by customers
who voted for Ike. Potatoes slide down like
triple cream in search of cardiac arrest.
Veggie casserole and nutrient-free green
beans dished by our robust waitress (without
tattoos) who lives just across the road.
Vegetable refills upon request. Coffee
black as a death wish to wash down pies
of every local fruit and berry.

No credit cards accepted.

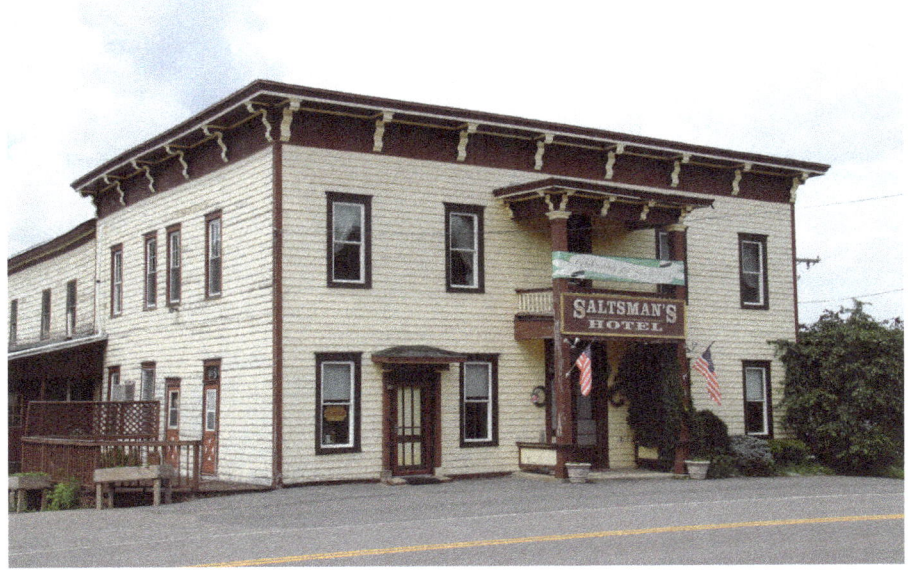

BULB PLANTING
—for Mary

Our young neighbor two doors distant
down the street is planting bulbs
beneath her leafless, aging maple.
In a normal year the ground
would be snow- or ice-capped,
her steel hole-in-one planter
hung up for winter on an angled nail
in the tool shed to grow spots of rust
about its seam and cutting edge.

But today the weather broke warm.
Out-of-season breezes nudged her
out of house, a sporty baseball cap
atop her head, her slender figure
wrapped in bright autumn plaid.
Kneeing earth, half blended with it,
she dreams while poking patiently
for soft soil pockets between webs
of root thin as children's fingers,
tough as grandmother hands.

She's planting crocuses, narcissus,
daffodils of sheer muslin, streaked
satin, glistening silk. She's intent
on protecting sheathed colors yet to be:
creams richer than English Devon,
yellows brighter than Saharan suns,
reds deeper than any rose can be.

She must know she may or may not
ever see the births of her midwifery,
her cap covering a shaven head,
her mackinaw a body worn thin
by radiation, chemotherapy.

But she continues willfully
feeling for those places where
the ground gives less stubbornly.
When she finds them she cuts a hole,
sets a bulb upright, covers it
gently, as if she's imitating
with attentive eye, caring
hand, the most graceful act
this living earth can offer.

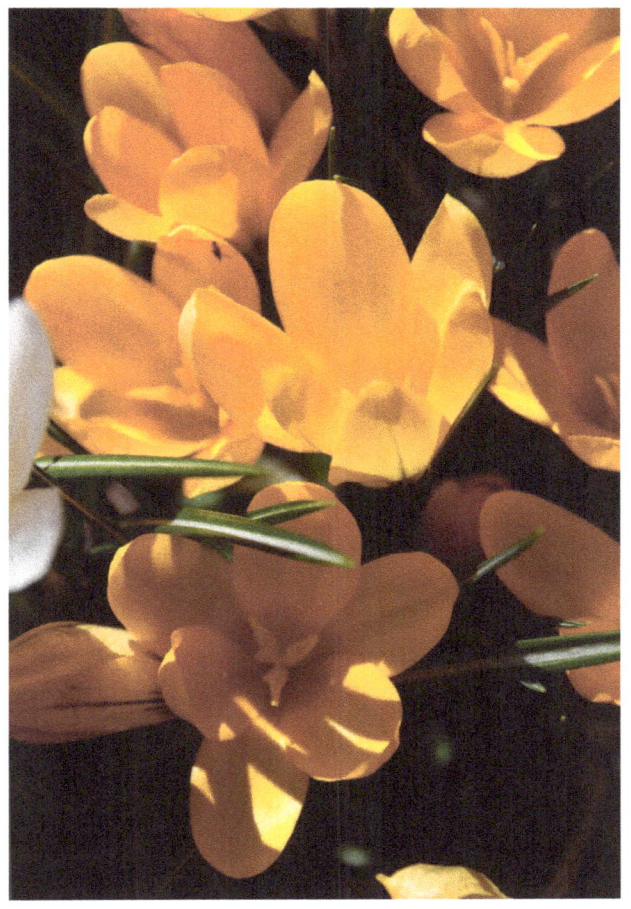

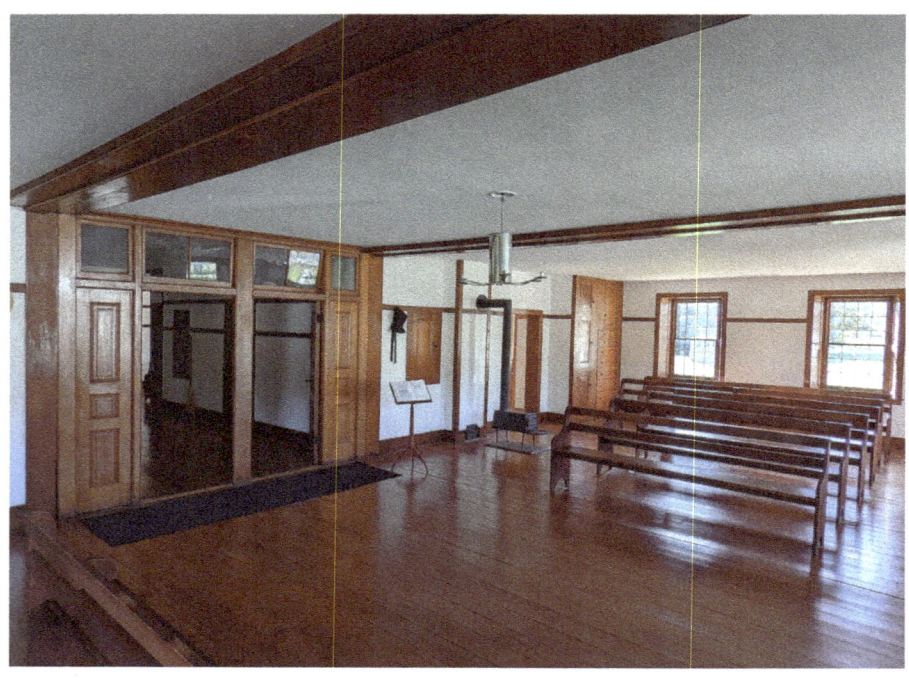

HARPING IN NEW LEBANON

*"... in my pictures I want to say something
consoling, as music does."*

—Vincent van Gogh

Once the sound of raucous voices
with hearts in Godly praise
filled this Shaker Meeting Room
and shook its floor with dances.
Wild men and frenzied women
separate in fevered unison.

Tonight we pass through one
main door to watch a woman waltz
her harp. She sits Buddha-still,
Buddha-silent, until with gentle
hands she draws her partner
to her waiting shoulder.

Aglow alike with surface light
the two begin their patterned
dance, their give and take of strings
strung taut and nimble fingers.
Each instrument true to itself
in need for more than self.

As she plays it and it plays her
strict figures melt in human sounds
to speak a love that resonates
through wood and flesh together.
A concert of simple gifts
well-given, well-received.

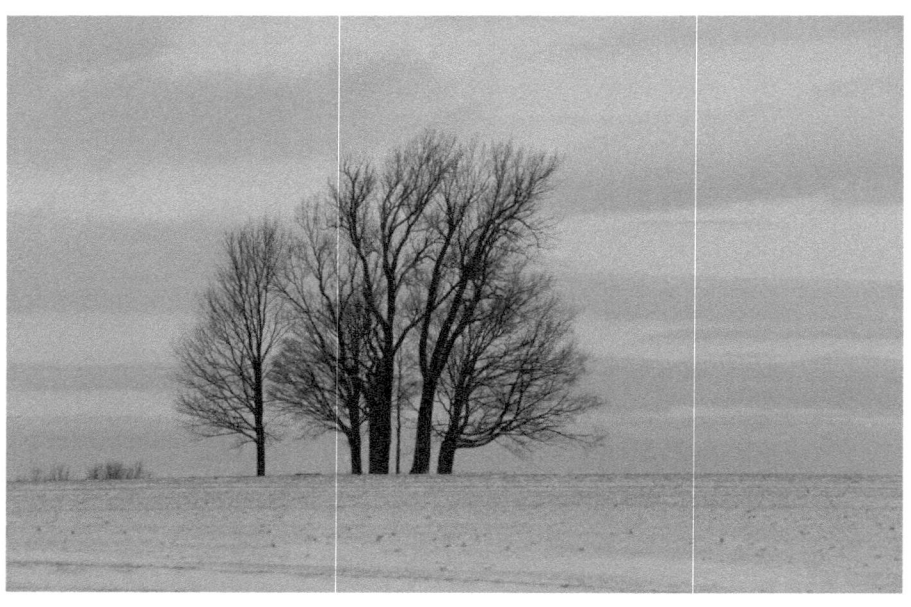

IN THE FIELD
—for Carl

The naturalist knows his territory,
his mote of our universe. Hay
fields now snowfields, he scans
land like a crow eyeing shed
corn from on high and like
a horned lark pecking for seeds
barely seeable in brown turf
beside sand shoulders of roads.

He notes Ron Myers' home turning
skeletal board by board, beamed
barns collapsing from indifference,
new hilltop homes—carbuncles
the locals call them—inflaming
earth's skin and deeper tissue.

He stands apart with an old red
maple taking it all in and bounds
like a jay from neighbor to neighbor
to ask about local legends, the lows
and highs of land, family histories,
Mrs. Marconi and her 35 cats. All
learning sweet as Rulison honey spun
from combs at the apiary down the road.

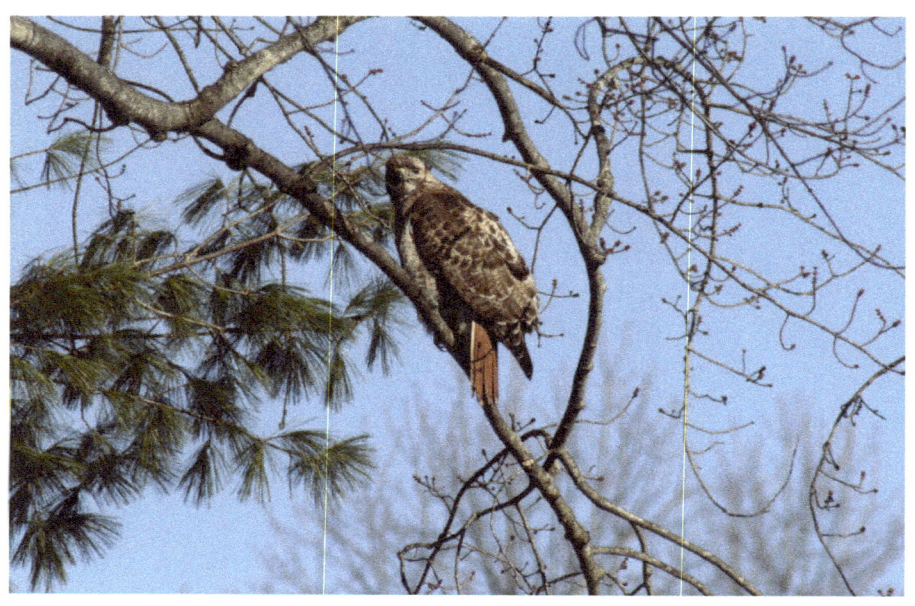

RED-TAILED

When boughs bare I see perched hawks
more easily, their rusty tails
like closed hand fans more clearly.
Only in winter are the two of us
together silent as snowfields.
I like to look them in the eye,
feel chuffed when they look back,
like to see their heads swivel
in slow motion, their eyes blaze
like holly berries. And I love
to watch their chests fill and bodies
crouch before they open and spread
barred wings in flight for mate or prey.

MURDER IN THE GRAVEYARD

Cemetery crows at dusk fill the sky
in corridors of communal flight
like swarming gnats, head for burial
ground roosts shrieking like hounds
at hell's gate until they perch mute
and motionless on twiggy boughs.

Aroused by scattered caws they explode
again in the waning light like a spray
of shrapnel, scramble like fighter jets
high above headstones, spread splayed wings
and cry against day's end as the sky turns
as black as their star-flecked bodies.

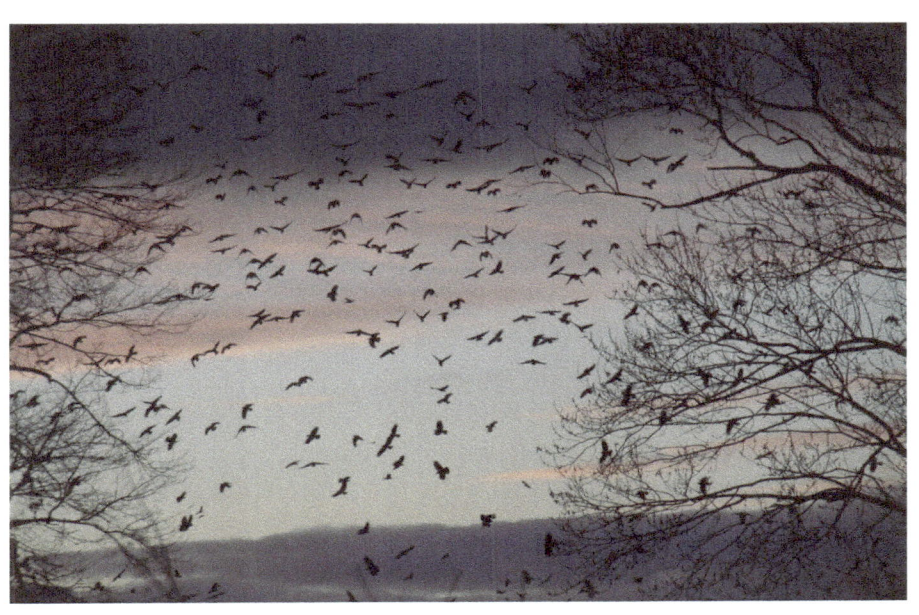

MOMENTARY ALIGNMENT

Zero hour frozen.
Gaping moon pure ultra white
nestled in black boughs.

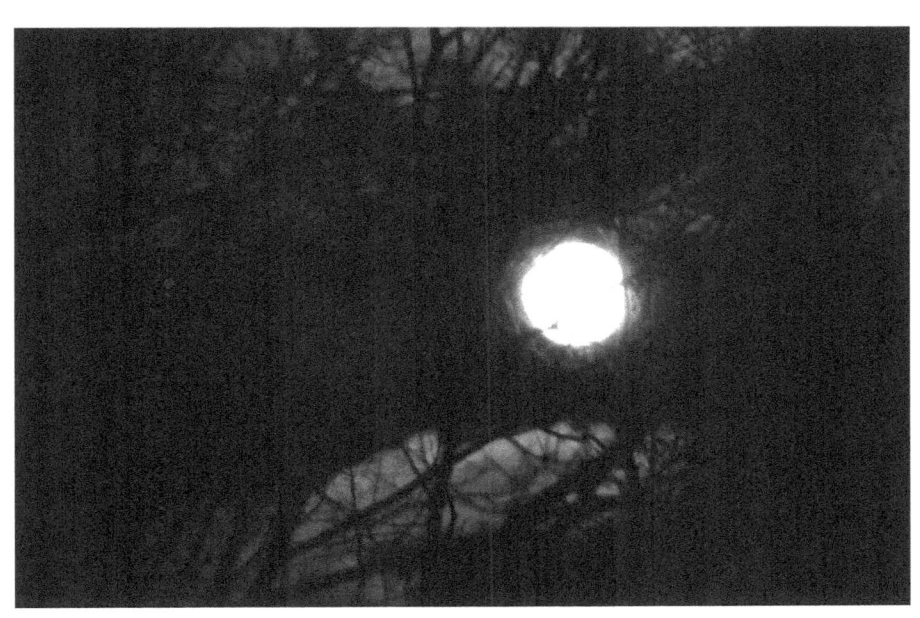

LIGHTNING STRIKE
—*for David*

After lightning struck our home
a friend wrote "everything now
will be before and after." But we
don't want that. We're looking hard
for continuity, yet can't see beyond
'what if,' 'what happened,' 'why us.'
High resolution pictures of imagined
loss cut into us like carbon knives.
Eight generations of curled photos
turned toxic fumes, penned letters
to and from loved ones reduced to ash.
One mother's father-made hope chest
become charred crate, two molded
portrait masks of who we were melted.
We think we're doing all we can
but have failed to blank out these
images and the memories of charcoal
smears, droplets of shingle tar, soot,
the smell of smoke smoldering.

There's no logic to what happened
after the electrified sky and charged
wind passed. Trees stood straight again
breathing relief, the driveway dried,
the black sky recovered gray. Then
a deafening crack without echo,
a crop whip with one stunning snap
on the roof's back. No way to tell
if it arrived from earth or air, raced

hidden underground or exploded above trees
as an invisible clap of thunder. No way
to know if it hit the iron vent pipe
or shot straight to the peak of the roof.
We only know we're luckier than fires
that make tragic news. And we've become
believers in caprice, the terror it can
bring and the need to comb out—smooth
as one can—tightly knotted changes
that split heavens, tear hearts.

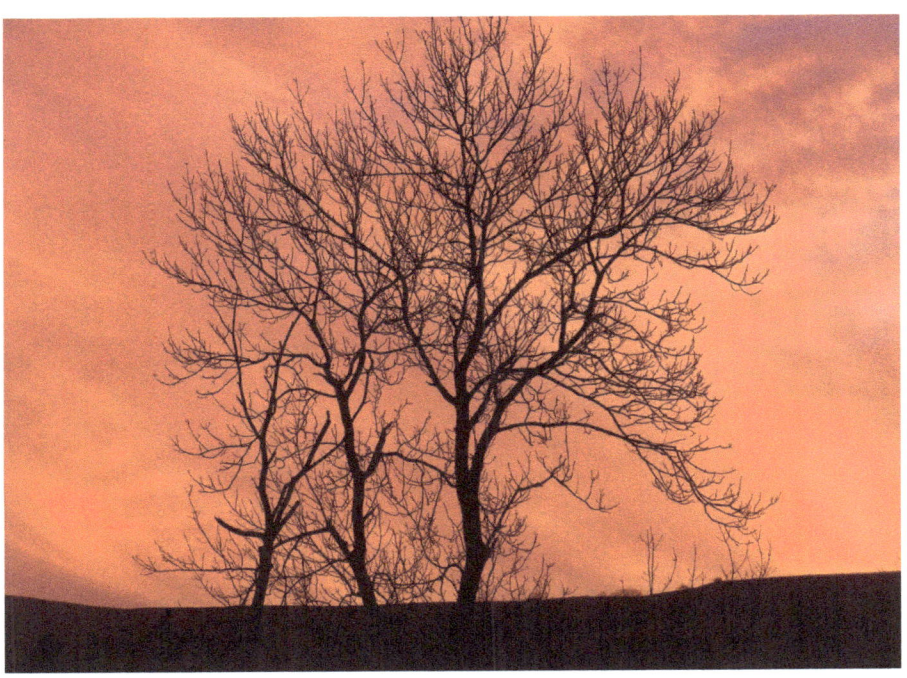

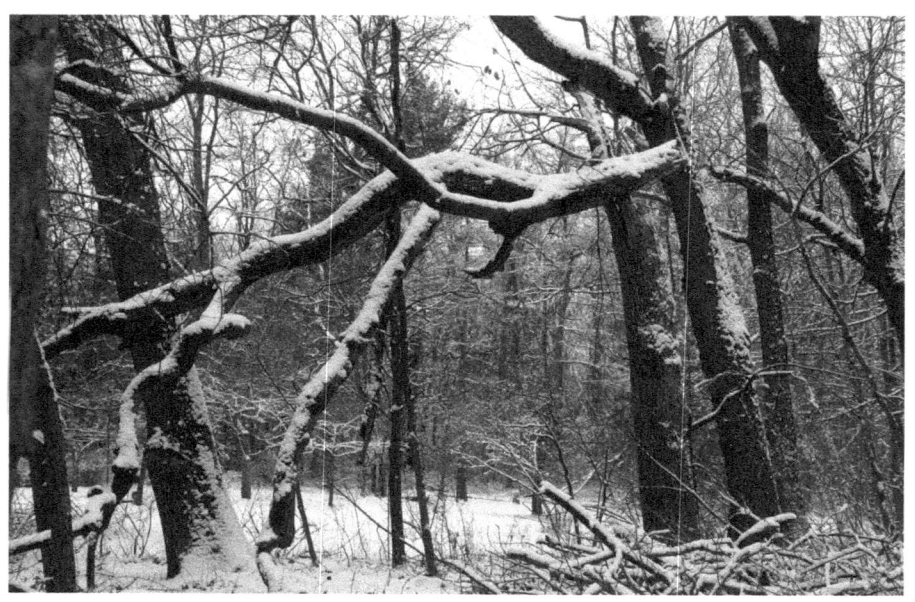

EVEN OAK

Northeast tempests
torture yearly our red oak
with sadistic pleasure.
The wind peppers trunks
like an assault rifle
on fully automatic. Limbs
sheathed in ice snap
like the crack of bullets.
Crowns shatter; racked
branches rip from sockets;
bark flays; ligaments
rupture and tendons tear
for sap letting. No sun
to salve. No breeze
to heal. In the omnipotent
heavens a frozen smile.

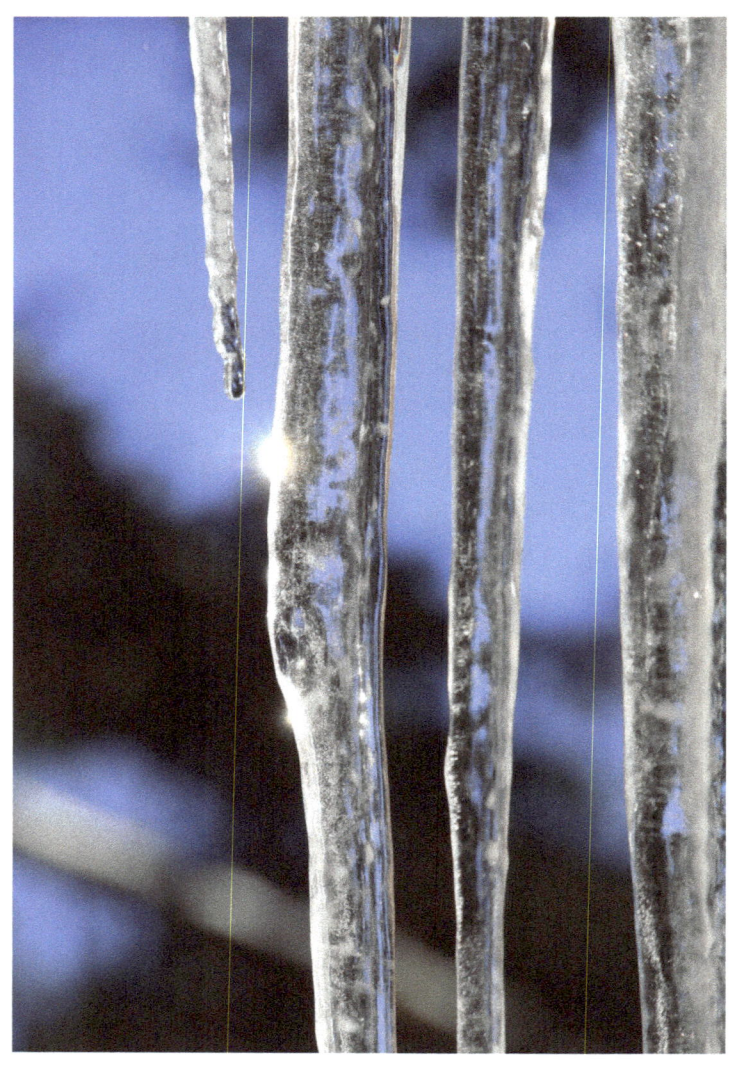

RETREAT

Where can one look?
Where can one go?

—when mantles of snow
freeze oaks; when young limbs
hang strait-jacketed in ice;
when powder snowfields harden
to slabs; when rows of woodlands
become funeral curtains; when
the indifferent sky opens its
frigid roof; when every star
shoots to earth arrows of icicles;
when the moon's sliver of an eye
closes to you in the night?

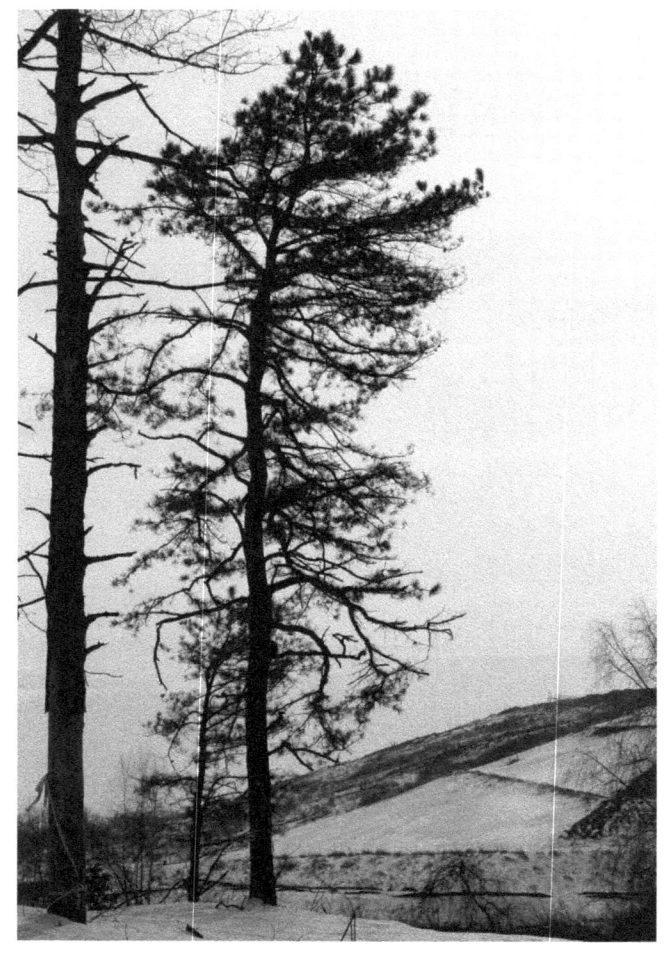

FIRST SNOW IN THE PINE BARREN

No chance for a raging wildfire
to purify on a day like this.
No red dragon to flame cones,
no scorched earth to renew.

Sky a gray void.

Dry lakebed packed with snow.

Paths slick as ice rinks.

Trees marked for death.

Live pitch pines hunger for fire,
scales on cones anxious to open,
seeds restless for conflagration.

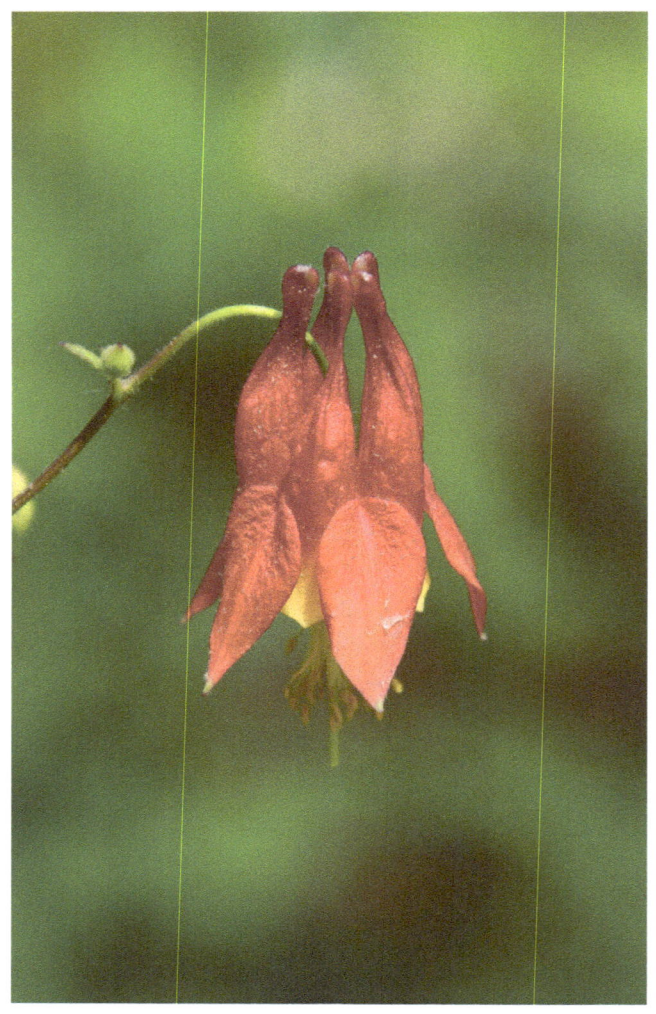

ILL-TEMPERED PRAYER

I'm sick of absolute zero in my bones.

Leaves of grass frozen beneath snow fields,
sprigs encased in blocks of ice,
bite of Antarctic air.

May so-called winter white
burn red devil in hell
so fruitful earth can warm again
with the colors of Adirondack
blue iris,
pink lady slipper,
red columbine.

ORCHARD PLANS

We'll put the orchard in this spring.
Although the season's not the best
we'll plant it then because it's been
too long. Nine years and nine friends
gone, the time has come to try to right
what's been upset, to fill our loss
with something found, fill emptiness
with buds and sprouts and fruit. We've
shopped with care, ordered strong,
lean saplings from a tree farm far north
that nurtures breeds to bear full fruit
in five to seven years. With luck
our neglected field will give soft way
in early May and our bin of compost smell
like earth we haven't smelled for half a year.
The trees will come as wispy shoots,
as two foot infants with elfin leaves.
We'll blend manure with clay and sand
for holes three deep, five feet across,
to make a roomy bed for roots as thin
as thread. Then bury screens of finest
mesh to keep burrowers out and hang cubes
of Irish Spring to try to detour deer.
We've plotted all the trees just so
to give them room to breathe and stretch,
yet know we'll likely shift our plans
when melting snow gives way to rock.
Knowing, too, New England practicality
shuns southern ornamentality, we've chosen
only varieties to suit our clime—
apple, cherry, peach, and pear. No nuts
or crabapples, we laugh, and no need
for plastic tags to pin down which is who.
Two fathers, two mothers, a favorite aunt,
four friends, the love each gave in their
own way deep-rooted in each and both of us.

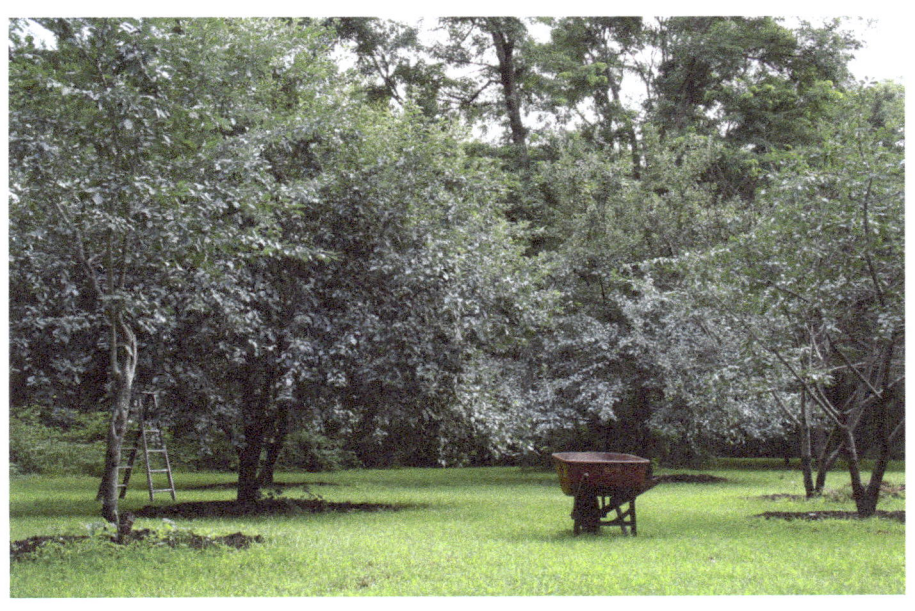

WEST AND EAST

THE DIFFICULTY OF DIVIDING DAY FROM NIGHT

The night before the bombs fell
on Iraq we stood in silence
darkly to hold a slender candle
white as peace in our hands.

The cool wind blew slight.
Our flame shivered against it
but cupped hands kept it alight.
Black dots of burned wick swam
in its wax pool like floaters
in an aging eye. A few spread
into worms or water snakes.

Back home we blew the candle out,
switched the porch light on.

Early next morning—the first day
of spring—our porch light bulb
dangled from its socket on filament
threads, its protective casing
shattered by a heavy human blow.
Wedges of glass lay scattered on ground
barely readying itself for life.

We felt we'd returned to that first
darkness on the face of the deep.
No hovering spirit was in sight,
no one calling for light. We felt
we'd fallen into a void blacker
even than the one that can't
distinguish wrong from right.

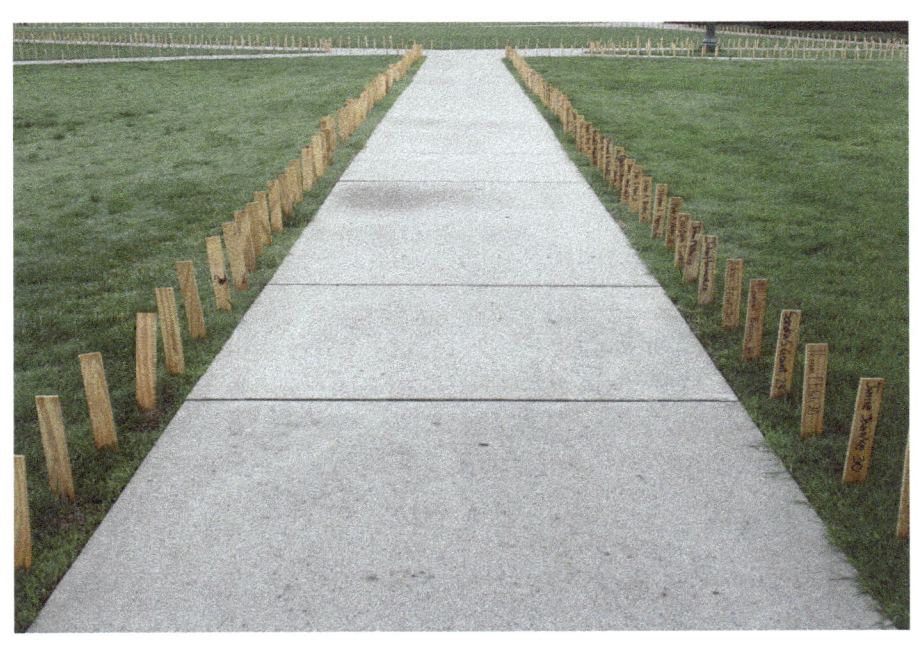

EYEING THE SEA

We circle the sun with false certainty, plant roots
with expectation of surety. The sea colorless as shattered
glass speckled by light teaches an elemental lesson
to do its best to keep us more honest. Forever changeable,
capricious, explosive as a geyser is what I found spying
through a knothole in a rock at Montaña de Oro. These days
there's no calm ebb and flow like a cradle for the earth,
it stirred to rage by winds that writhe like hunted Leviathans.
Its head spins and gasps for air, belly wrenches with toxins
and sewage. Skies overdose on fuel and wildfires. Water and air
transform into a vengeful eye with eyewalls to strike terror,
drown human pride, wash clean our world of human wreckage.

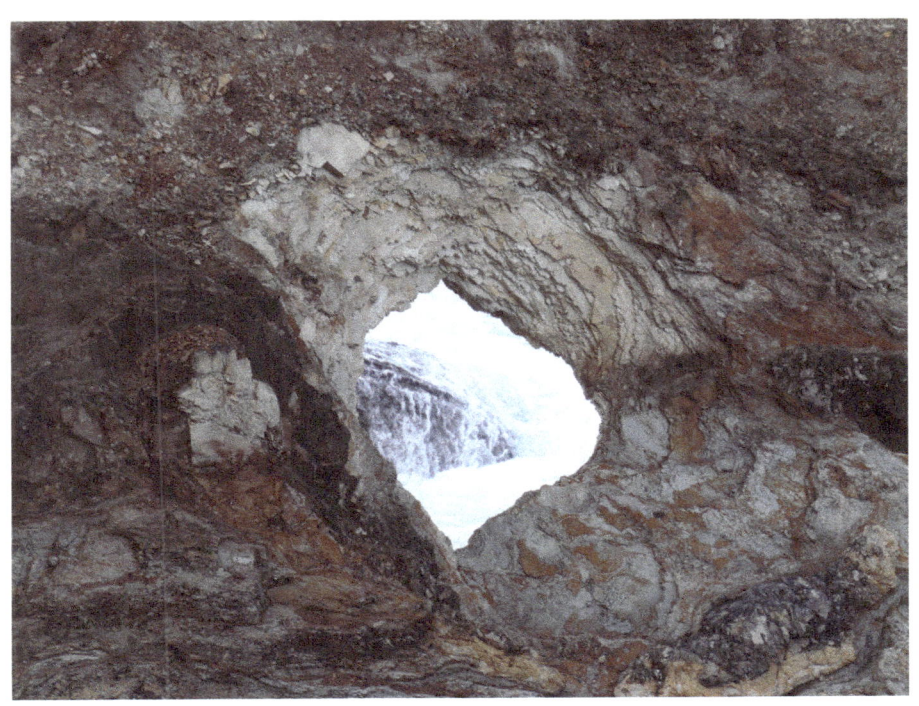

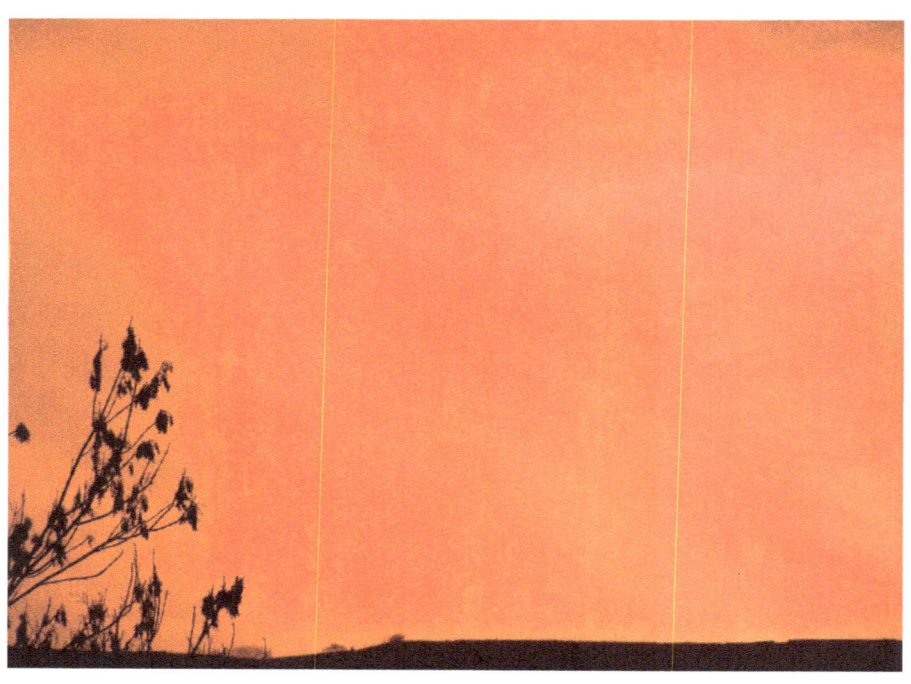

LATE SUMMER BLUES
—after Robert Johnson

I went to the crossroad, fell down on my knees,
I went to the crossroad, fell down on my knees,
Asked the Lord above to comfort me please.

Leaves tremblin' on trees, wind in a gale,
A fire breathin' hellhound on my trail,
My soul burnin' up, my body gone pale.

The world hot as an old blast furnace,
The world on fire like an old blast furnace,
The world in flames to burn us, burn us.

No ice in the house to chill my bones,
No ice in the graveyard, just crossbones,
No ice nowhere, the earth scorched stone.

Red sun risin' up, red moon goin' down,
Red moon risin' up, red sun goin' down,
All green turned black in Memphis town.

Once the devil come knockin', knockin' at my door,
Once the devil come knockin', knockin' at my door,
That devil don't need to knock no more.

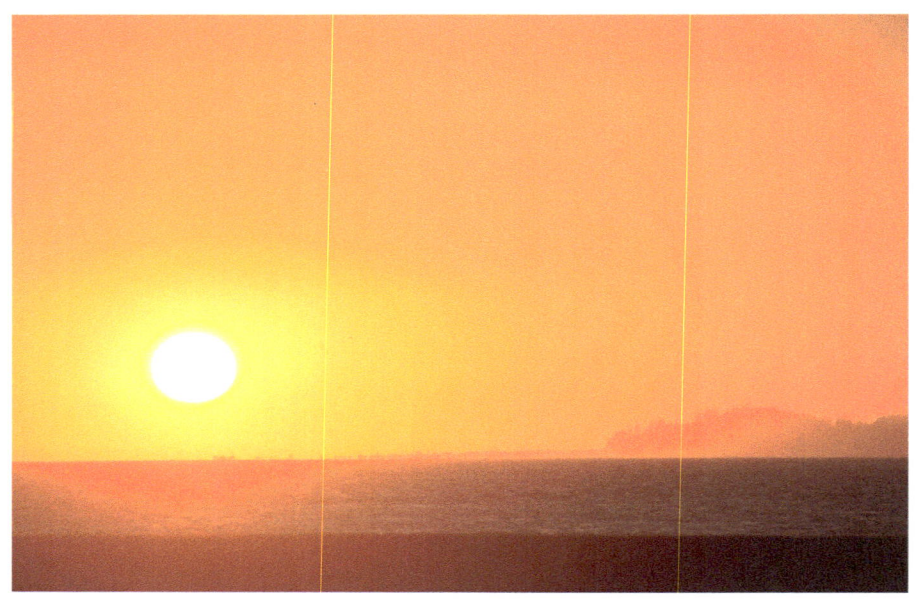

LESSON FOR SURVIVAL
—after Susan Barba

The granddaughter, who to her grandfather
is as beautiful as his sister was, asked him,
"Why is the sun fair?" Andranik Vartanian
answered, "Because it shines down equally
on everyone." He said this to her when
she was a teenager ready to free herself
from shadows. He a survivor of the Armenian
genocide. He the boy who buried in the sands
of Honey River his father stripped naked
by Kurds. He who scavenged for Turks pieces
of gold and silver in houses laid waste,
burnt-out barns, on corpses, to save his life.
He who killed his boyhood friend because luck
put in his hand the gun with one bullet. He
who fingered water drop by drop onto the burning
lips of a man with ribs sliced by a hatchet
and watched him cry and cry, then die. He the boy
who knew his country like the five fingers
in front of his eye: ditches, bushes, forests,
deep rivers to hide in, mountains to flee to.

I must ask you, Andranik, how can you say
the fair sun shines down equally on everyone?

WINTER DOWNTOWN

Across gunmetal gray State Street
a homeless man wrapped like a bundle
of sticks scrapes himself up hill
toward the County Court square
where a vigilant Union soldier
with set jaw lowers his head in thought
of comrades lost to single shots,
shrapnel, typhoid, history.

He looks up at the stone statue
with eyes dim as diminished cinders,
expression vacant as no man's land.
He unbraids his gnarled fingers,
ponders his palms of blue netting.
Overhead, a silver maple
with buds like sheathed sabers
dares to dream of leafing green.

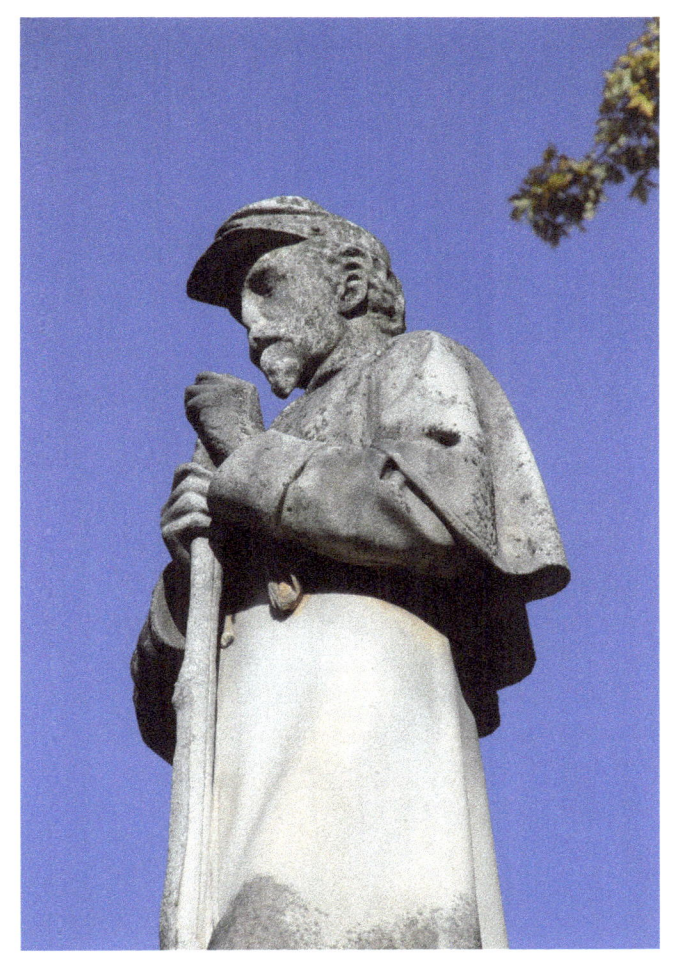

A WINTER TALE

Take a tip from Nature, I tell myself.
Flow with her flows, shift with her shifts,
change with her changes. The arrival
and departure of crocuses in spring,
marigolds in summer, monkshood in fall,
glories of the snow in winter. Keep rotating
like the earth, the sun, the moon. If I must
linger, I know to avoid winter's death trap.
Turns of seasons for my mother now invisible
to her hardened lenses. She's night-blind
to winter's slow-moving nourishment, numbers
her days to be in perfect rhyme with its
spasmic cold, longest night. Mind frozen,
heart iced at every visit. It's a state
of barely being I do not understand
and cannot accept. I need to imagine her free
from the struggle to find hope in erratic
flecks of light. And I need to steady myself
with metaphor to shield the pain.

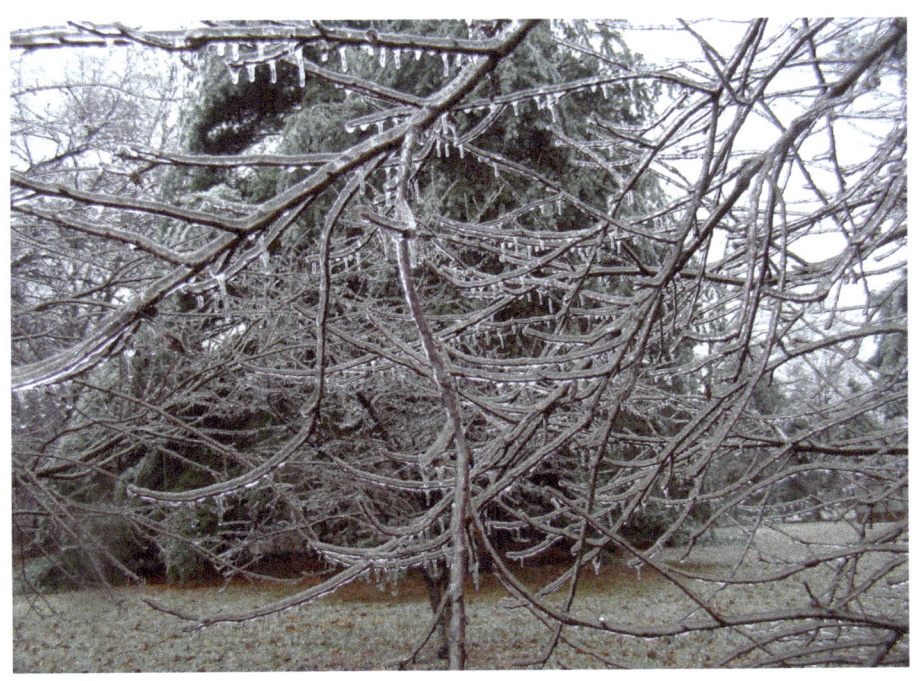

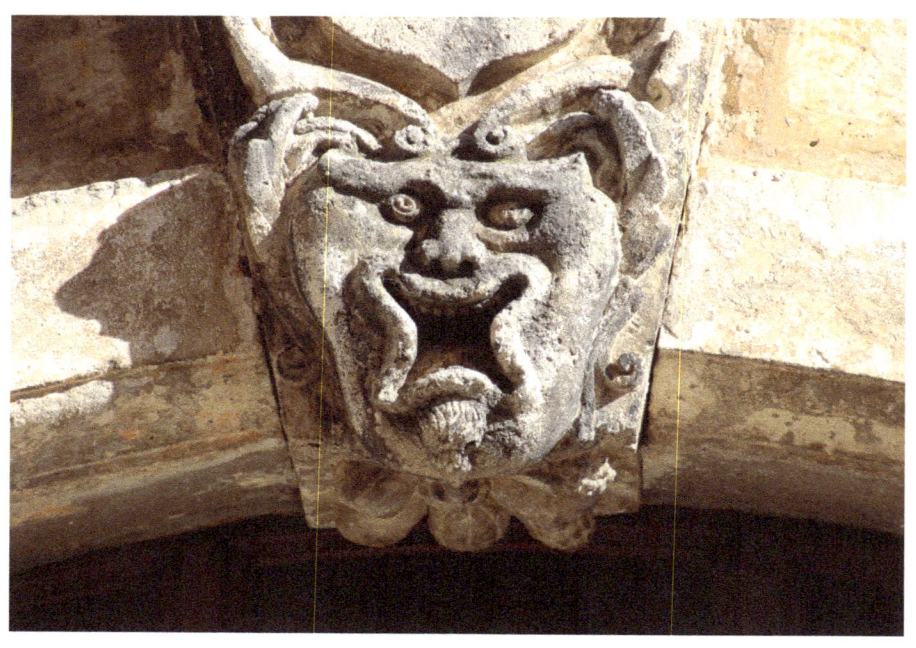

DEATH'S LIFE SPAN

It's best to forget about death's arrival,
best to stop thinking its presence into being.
Though it's only hiding, to a child it's nowhere
to be found. It might be sleeping deeper
than a soul, or lighting a universe beyond
human sight. When found, as one day it must be,
death can terrify, like meeting a weaving
semi-truck on a one-lane road, or like imagining
the tip of a stiletto pressed against the iris
of one eye. Only when accepted can death be
a beast at rest far distant in tall grass.

PITCH PINE

Imagine a tree bedded
down in sand and fed
on a steady diet of it,
roots feasting on grains
washed down with spring
thaw, summer rains. Such
makes for thick plates
of bark and for sharp
needles of forest green.

Until, that is, needles
ignite, bark flames
from life-giving fire
and cones sealed tight
explode like grenades,
scatter to indifferent
winds seeds in search
of toeholds in acidic,
unfruitful barrens.

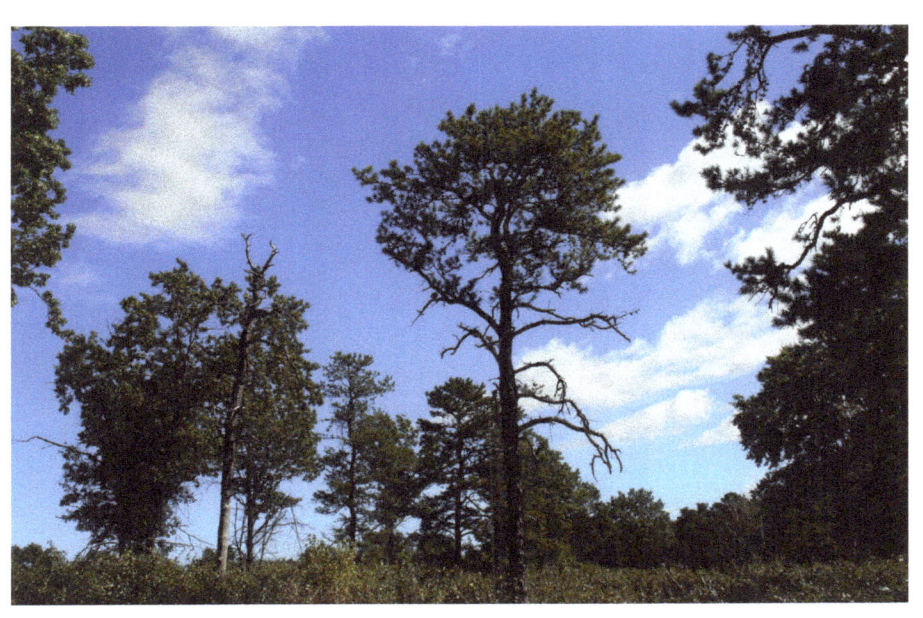

UNUSED RED BARN

"Barn red," I learned
 from a house painter,
 was an Indian mix
 of cow's milk and cow's

 blood, the pale white
 enriched by the marriage,
 the deep, congealing red
 thinned by it. A true

 sacrifice, I thought,
 the milk of bovine
 kindness blended with
 the blood of slaughter.

 Or maybe no sacrifice at all,
 simply animal giving way
 to Puritan practicality.
 This faded, rotting barn

 now a carcass of veins
 daubed unintentionally
 with a small taste of life,
 a faint smell of death.

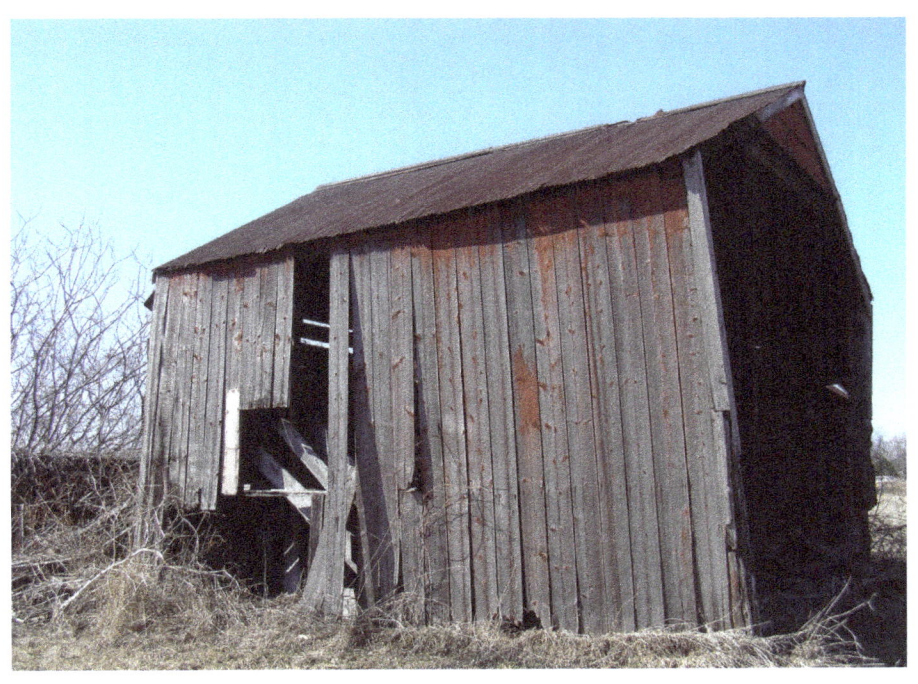

MAN OF SORROWS

To remind me of this man
a potted Crown of Thorns
grows near my windowsill
in indirect light. Thorns

sharp as iron spikes run
the length of gray-skinned
stems hidden by umbrellas
of leaves at top. Tiny

trinkets of gold blossom
on slender threads. Red bracts
open like butterfly wings.
If broken or cut, the hearts

of stalks gush thin, watery,
poisonous white milk until
they seal themselves, heal
themselves, with thick balm.

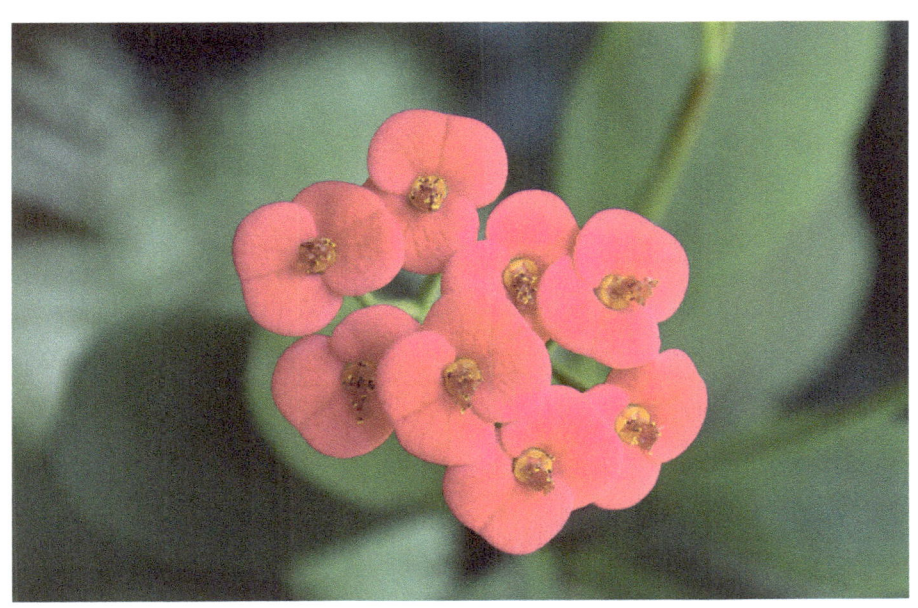

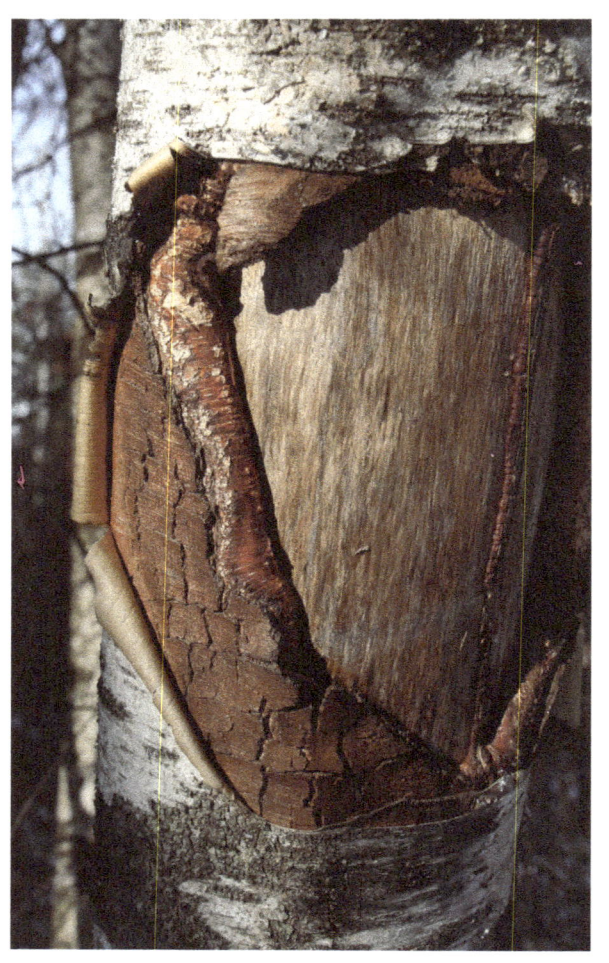

RECOVERY

It's not a pretty sight
but this birch is alive.
Sternum sawed open,
bark cage spread, veins
harvested for arterial
grafting. All readied
for a bypass, its heart
refusing to not beat.

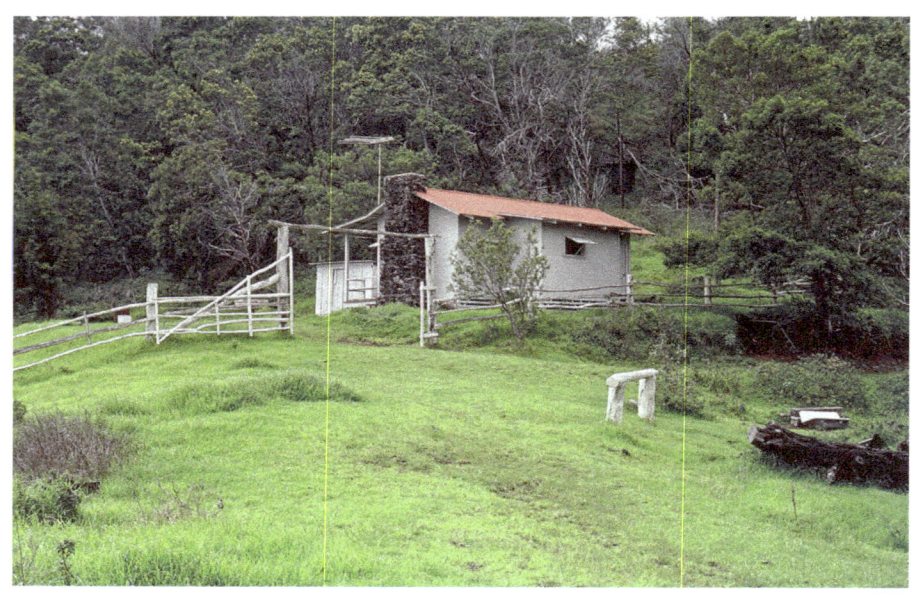

MAUI
—for Shawne

On a dusty hillside road
two miles from the unpaved
main road sits our cabin on posts
and piers. Its metal roof a sun
shield, its walls light as balsa.
When we open the door cockroaches
greet us with toenail scurries.

Far below us La Perouse Bay
with shore lava black, splintered
as a devil's tooth. Beyond the bay
the island sacred as an ocean deity
now desolate, uninhabited. Its cliffs
torpedoed by submarines and heart
bombed to death for war preparations.

Near our house an arboretum
of indigenous flora in a volcanic
hollow. In our yard a pony to ride
for our daughter and carnations
in bloom all year. Drunk on their own
fragrance they reel with the same joy
we feel in our threadbare home.

THAI LEAVES
—for Eric

"We are here to see things as they are."
—SAYING PINNED TO A TREE IN WAT PAH NANACHAT

Leaves break free from trees and fall through every Asian season in the monastery of Wat Pah Nanachat. At dawn and dusk robed monks sweep stone squares, sand pathways, garden grass. They hold in hands softened by prayer the bamboo handles of brooms to sweep and clear, clear and sweep. With each step their bodies sway to the music of palm leaf bristles on stone, sand, grass. Monks eye each leaf that falls, hear every sweep of broom while mosquitoes buzz about them, dogs bark in the distance. Leaves once green pale, curl, brown on the ground. Nature a patient teacher, monks patient learners. This simple act fills them with pleasure, fills them with understanding, fills them with acceptance. They smile in the open air, their lives like leaves breathing.

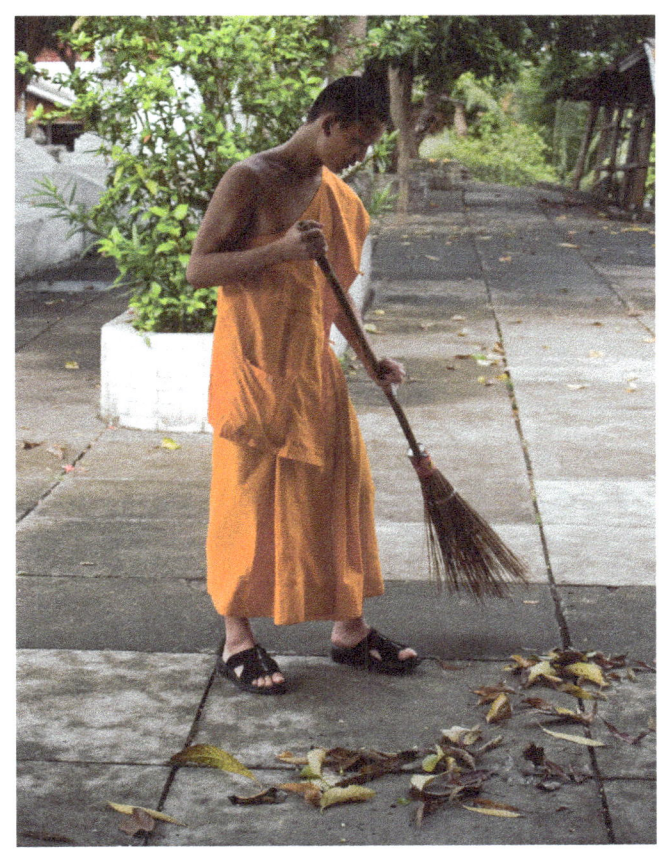

NIGHT AND DAY NEAR CAPE DISAPPOINTMENT

Starless dome by night
dome of cloud by day
can make a soul
in an outworn lighthouse
feel shrouded by nightmares
where demons of the mind
breed despair.

But a soul pressed
by these same skies
can turn eyes inward
where there's no enclosure or closure,
where compassion and wisdom
radiate as suns
illuminate together.

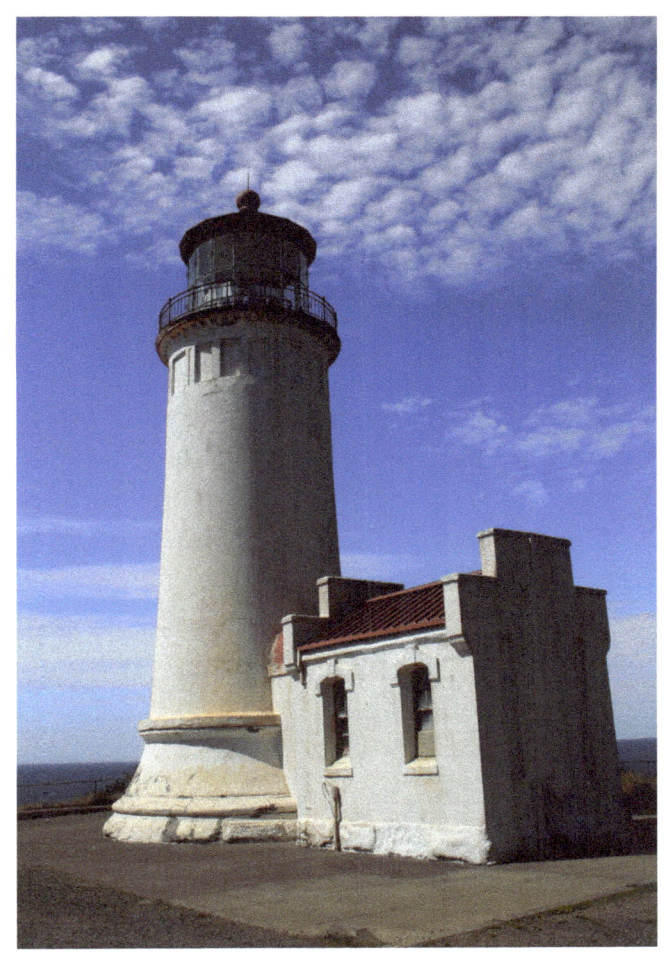

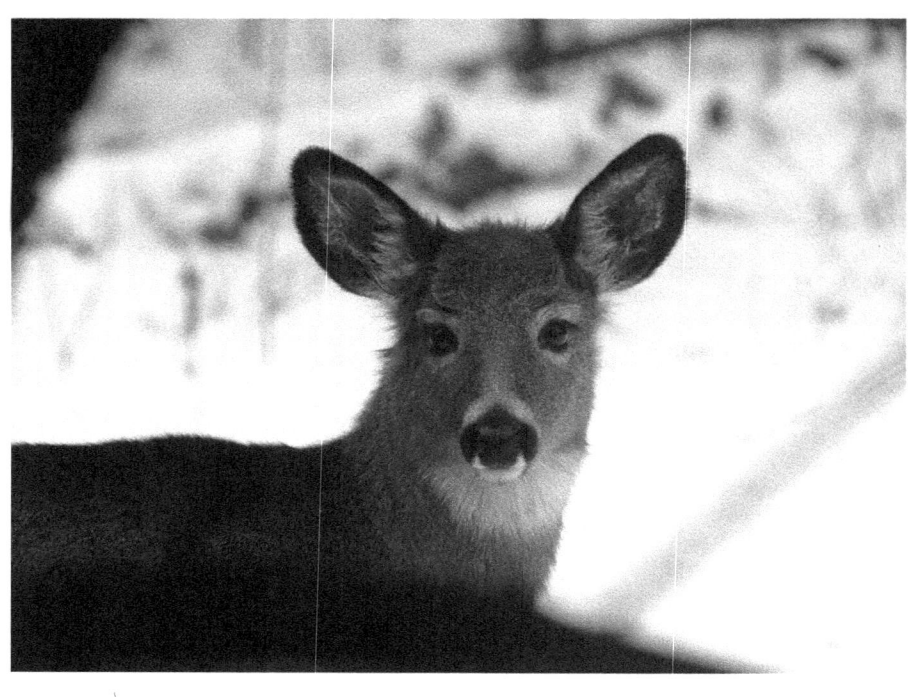

SUBURBAN DEER

> "...faith from the Pali... is saddha, which
> literally means 'to place the heart upon.'"
>
> —Sharon Salzberg

The damn deer nearly killed
all ten of our mature yews
when we were away last winter.
It wasn't good enough, it seems,
for coolheaded seasoned vets
and cocky young bucks to simply
bed down under the oldest
and nibble midnight snacks.

From mowed field to empty house
every branch they could neck
stripped bare, tooth marks left
like notches on a bedpost. Dawn
and dusk I'd seen them beyond
human smell and rifle range
tongue blades of meadow grass,
nibble dandelions, mouth healthy-
hearted berries, acorns, windfall
apples. But never our yews.

I later learned from neighbors
the pond had been low and dry
like no winter before, parched reeds
spindly as newborn fawns crackling
in the wind like cornhusks. Shame
chilled my body, burned my eyes,
filled my throat with ash. Then
saddha opened like a hidden spring
and empathy drowned my thirst.

THE FOREST REFUGE IN JANUARY
". . . awareness is a refuge"
—AMARO BHIKKHU

The world moves like winter waters—
fast and fearful as southern torrents,
slow and easy as southwestern creeks,
hidden as northeastern streamlets
that start and stop in air pockets
beneath ice sheets thin as wax paper.

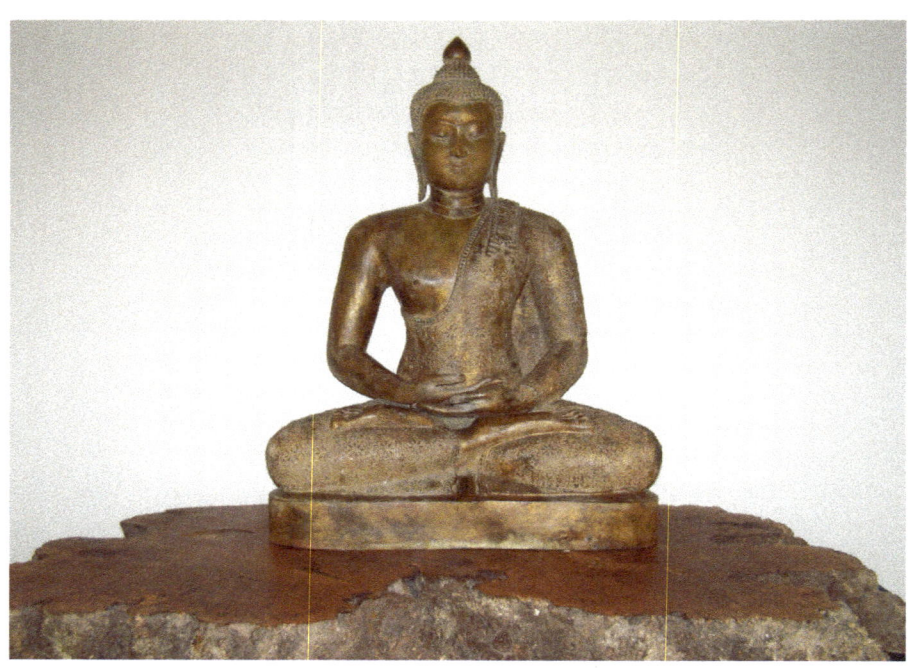

Here in Barre the world often seems
not to move at all, like ice falls
frozen over roadside granite boulders.
But it does move, quietly as melting
snow from trunks of pine and surely
as awareness stirring from slumber
to nudge pavement stones askew.

Last night's snow covers the refuge
this morning, a coat of powder
that is and is not water. To stay
warm yogis inside sit and walk, eat
and sleep, behind pillars of reclaimed
river logs hand-hewn and varnished
for long-life surrounded by windows
cleared of frost by first sunlight.

In the hall deep inside they meditate
in the presence, in the company,
of a Buddha of Thai wood. He, too,
is like winter water: frozen and fluid,
still and still moving. The rock pedestal
he sits on is immovable, a foundation
for thought set half outside the building,
half in. Half to draw the outside world in,
half the inside world out. At the rock's
core a waking heart unbinds itself from fire
and becomes a fountain of spring waters.

BIOGRAPHIES

JIM MCCORD is a former teacher whose poems have appeared in a variety of journals and six books. The three most recent books pair poems with photographs by Carol McCord.

CAROL MCCORD is a lifetime hiker and former Yoga instructor whose photographs have been selected for exhibitions and publications in the United States and abroad. Her special interests are the worlds of nature, history, art, and architecture.

Shanti Arts

Nature ▪ Art ▪ Spirit

Please visit us online
to browse our entire book catalog,
including poetry collections and fiction,
books on travel, nature, healing, art,
photography, and more.

Also take a look at our highly regarded art
and literary journal, *Still Point Arts Quarterly*,
which may be downloaded for free.

www.shantiarts.com